AF386370

Through Fire and Sky
Volume II

Contents

Foreword

It is a delight to introduce you to the second volume of the wartime memoirs of the distinguished soldier and aviator Karl Knoblauch. He had a particularly interesting war, serving from 1939 to 1945 in the west and east, on the ground and in the air. For the account of his busy war up to 1944, I thoroughly recommend you start with Knoblauch's *Through Fire and Sky, Volume I* (first published in German in 1992 as *Zwischen Metz und Moskau – Between Metz and Moscow*), which will set the scene for this book, although you can equally read *Through Fire and Sky, Volume II* as a standalone series of remembrances and impressions. This tome is a faithful translation of Knoblauch's *Dem Ende entgegen* (*Towards the End*), first published in Germany also in 1992.

Knoblauch was active in old comrades' associations into the 1980s and pieced together this record from his old maps, photographs, letters and the diary he kept from 1938, where his powers of close observation speak loudly. Both volumes contain many personal photographs and paperwork related to his wartime career and decorations. This is rare because most awards and documents were lost or confiscated during the process of becoming a prisoner of war. In Knoblauch's case, he was lucky to be able to deposit many personal items and his diary at his family home during several leaves from the front. Both original books of memoirs were self-published by the enterprising old soldier from his home in Ronnenberg, near Hanover, before they were picked up by commercial publishing houses.

By the end of Volume I, Herr Knoblauch had been awarded an Iron Cross, Second Class, in France (11 July 1940), gained the same in First Class (27 March 1942), an Aircrew Clasp in successively Bronze, Silver and Gold (the last awarded on 21 February 1943 for 110 missions), a Luftwaffe Honour Goblet (29 March 1943) and the German Cross in Gold (17 October 1943), only a notch below a Knight's Cross. In May 1943 Feldwebel (Sergeant) Knoblauch was commissioned as a *Leutnant* (pilot officer), which together with the Russian Front Medal (5 August 1942) and a Silver Wound Badge (14 October 1943) spell out a busy war. His activities in Volume II will see him promoted to *Oberleutnant* (first lieutenant) (22 November 1944) and bring him a rare Luftwaffe Ground Assault Badge (12 December), collectively qualifying him to bring the reader unique insights into the nature of German ground and air combat throughout 1939–45.

Born on 24 June 1921 and brought up near Hanover, firm-of-jaw and athletic, Knoblauch realised he was no scholar; he enjoyed the outdoor life and undertook basic training in the Reich Labour Service. Then, against his father's wishes, young Karl voluntarily enlisted in the German army. He was soon posted to the bicycle reconnaissance troop of General Sixt von Armin's 95th Infantry Division as a young trooper and junior NCO. Of particular value to the reader, he records his training courses and preparatory exercises, both as an embryonic infantryman and later as an aerial observer; in most World War II memoirs these aspects are glossed over in the hurry to tell the story of battle.

From these details, we learn much of Knoblauch, his comrades and the institutions he serves. His bicycle unit crossed the Franco-German border on 16 May 1940 and served opposite the Maginot Line in eastern France, between Metz and Saarbrucken, south of the panzer breakthroughs in 1940, trading tentative shots with nervous Frenchmen until the June armistice. Such was his affection towards his old division (he would visit them when his Luftwaffe unit was stationed in Smolensk in the summer of 1943) that he later wrote an account of their history in France and Russia (*Kampf und Untergang der 95. Infanteriedivision*, published in German in 2008).

Had Knoblauch stayed with the division, he would almost certainly have lost his life or been captured in its many battles on the Eastern Front, as happened to his former comrades of those days. It was eventually destroyed near Vitebsk, north-east Belarus, during the Red Army's Operation 'Bagration' of June 1944. However, in late 1940 Knoblauch had put his name forward for aerial observer/photographer training and spent the next seven months learning his new trade in Reichenberg in what was then Sudetenland, now Liberec in Czechia, and Grossenhain airbase in Saxony, followed by a final two months based at Nohra aerodrome, near Weimar. Close to the latter was Buchenwald concentration camp, which was partly concealed by a wood of beech trees, but not to a trained observer in the sky. Yet not a mention does it get.

Knoblauch was given leave back to Hanover from 27 November to 8 December 1941, when his father was dangerously ill and died of natural causes, a privilege accorded to few warriors in the midst of war.

Knoblauch was then deployed to a Junkers-88-equipped long-range recon-naissance squadron, based in and around Smolensk, in the central sector of the Eastern Front. With his portable camera and notebook, Knoblauch was a key member of the four-man crew, monitoring Soviet troop concentrations along roads and railways, up to 500km from the front and sometimes as far as Moscow. They frequently supported ground units in the German-held Rzhev salient, to their north and occupied by Walter Model's Ninth Army of Günter von Kluge's Army Group Centre. For further context, Prit Buttar's *Meat Grinder: The Battles for the Rzhev Salient 1942–43* (2022) provides greater insight into this punishing 1942–43 campaign. Knoblauch's valuable written and verbal reports, submitted immediately on landing, along with his photographs, contributed to the Luftwaffe's operational, rather than tactical, intelligence picture, in much the same manner that the Spitfires and Mosquitos of the RAF's Photo Reconnaissance Units similarly provided the British with knowledge of their opponents at this time.

Soon, Knoblauch had notched up 100 combat sorties, and the observant reader may detect a growing hint of tiredness that floats through his pages. Unlike his Allied counterparts there seems to have been little attempt to rest aircrew, and though he never mentions it, PTSD must have been there, too. The turn of the tide is obvious from the number of fellow crews who failed to return from missions, often attacked by Russian-piloted Hawker Hurricanes. These were some of the 3,000 of the type shipped via Arctic convoys into Murmansk from Britain, and thrown against the Luftwaffe with great success throughout 1942. With gut-wrenching frequency, Knoblauch notes whenever aircrew, close friends all, disappear over enemy territory. After 165 combat missions, his own time came on 2 September 1943 when his twin-engined aircraft was bounced by Russian fighters and he was wounded in the left collarbone, eye and lungs by bullets. His Ju 88 limped home with Knoblauch clinging to life and, after evacuation back to Germany by hospital train, he was nursed back to health until his eventual discharge from hospital on 9 August 1944. What happens next is the subject of this volume.

Knoblauch was highly intelligent and steered his own fate to a remarkable degree through the vicissitudes of the Third Reich at war. On leaving medical care, with a weakened left lung and blinded eye, his flying days were over, but he could not face inactivity. On 7 September 1944, he volunteered for ground combat duty and ended up in the Fallschirm-Panzergrenadierdivision 2 of the 'Hermann Göring' Panzer Corps. This was a late-war patchwork of surplus Luftwaffe personnel, founded on 24 September 1944 at Radom in Poland to fight alongside the Fallschirm-Panzerdivision 1 'Hermann Göring' in a corps-level formation. By then the 'Hermann Göring' Division had grown so large and unwieldy that it was split, also on 24 September, into a panzer (armoured) division and a panzer grenadier (armoured infantry) division, with other units added.

There was nothing remotely *Fallschirm* (parachute-trained) about any of these formations, but they satisfied Göring's empire-building ego and fought in terms of equipment and doctrine as army units, though wearing Luftwaffe insignia and nominally under air force control. As such, they were poured into the diminishing resources of the Wehrmacht against the crushing Soviet offensive in East Prussia of October 1944 to January 1945. Highly recommended is Prit Buttar's *Battleground Prussia* (2010), which provides a wider context to these bitter battles over what was then German terrain but is now part of Kaliningrad (Russia) and Poland. Unlike the much-documented Panzerdivision 'Hermann Göring', seasoned veterans of much fighting in the Mediterranean, there is no official history of its late-war *Panzergrenadier* cousin, so this volume of Knoblauch's memoirs also has the heady responsibility of plugging the gap in the official record.

After the briefest of refresher courses in infantry tactics, Knoblauch leaves for Warsaw and the Eastern Front on 30 September 1944 by *Fronturlauberzug* (express train for combat-bound personnel) and arrives to find everything in flux, the Russians advancing everywhere and his own division facing impossible odds. Quickly he is promoted from platoon to company commander and finally adjutant of the division's fusilier battalion. The new adjutant is perfectly at home in this role because of his previous infantry training and service with the 95th Division in 1939–40, and also his meticulous record-keeping as an aerial observer over Russia. This brings him a more panoramic awareness of the hopelessness of the Eastern Front in late 1944 than many colleagues would have possessed.

As forces on the *Westfront* attacked the Americans in the Ardennes, on 20 December 1944 he finds himself invited to express his views on the Stauffenberg bomb plot with his new commander, Captain August Wolf. Knoblauch is somewhat surprised, surmising, 'The staff of the battalion headquarters haven't yet discussed 20 July, its background, or its consequences. None of us knows each other well enough … truth be told, I am bothered by the fact that soldiers from old Prussian families broke their oath of allegiance.'

Wolf responds with extraordinary candour:

'Mr Knoblauch … the Führer … is not held aloft by the officer corps. Aside from a few exceptions, the officer corps primarily feels itself bound by duty to the Reich. I would go so far as to venture to say that the enormous sacrifices that have been made thus far were not for the Führer but rather for the survival of the Reich … Our duty, Mr Knoblauch, lies only to the Reich! … Let us make no mistake that the Russians will confront us in a final battle here in East Prussia in a few weeks. We will go into this battle despite knowing that most of us will not survive. Our actions will certainly not be determined by the oath that binds us to Hitler. We will stand and probably fall here in East Prussia because we want to defend the Reich and its people in a final act of soldierly duty against the Russians. This has nothing to do with the oath of allegiance. It is instead a matter of self-respect … Let us bring this topic of discussion to a close and conduct ourselves in future as if it had never taken place.'

'It never took place, Captain,' Knoblauch wisely replies (pp. 62–3).

Knoblauch and his men are immediately sucked into the swirling battle around Gumbinnen (today's Gusev, in Russian Kaliningrad), site of a major World War I battle, which had been captured by Soviet forces on 22 October 1944, was retaken by the Germans in late October, only to be reconquered by the Red Army during the great Soviet East Prussia offensive on 21 January 1945. He encounters Volkssturm units defending small hamlets. Of one forty-man unit, he asks about their principal weapon: 'Now tell me about that strange machine gun you have there.' He is left speechless at their response: 'This is a Belgian machine gun. Unfortunately, we don't have any Belgian ammunition' (p. 103).

On 25 January 1945, Captain Wolf is wounded and Knoblauch takes over the battalion, but within hours, he, too, is injured in close-combat fighting in a manor house near the hamlet of Hochlindenberg (now Podlipovo in Russian Kaliningrad). By lifts from passing vehicles, local trains and on foot, Knoblauch leads other walking wounded westwards; all the while his remaining strength is ebbing. On 5 February at Tiegenhof (now Nowy Dwór Gdański in northern Poland) he is told to dismount from his railway carriage. 'Fall in! Rank is irrelevant!' He finds a detail of the Waffen-SS stands at the end of the platform, submachine guns at the ready, looking for deserters. He observes, 'Anyone who doesn't have a wound tag is separated from the rest' (p. 124). Knoblauch presents the correct paperwork and is directed to board another train. He reaches Hamburg and relative safety on 10 February, managing a brief stint of home leave afterwards.

After leaving hospital from his second serious wounding, he leads a group of Luftwaffe men from Berlin across a collapsing Reich and it is remarkable to note how much of his travel is by train, despite the prevalence of Allied air supremacy. On 14 April, he witnesses his first sight of a jet fighter tearing into a gaggle of US Flying Fortresses, damaging or destroying three of them. 'I am mesmerised. I can clearly see that the German fighter has two engines. It is presumably a Messerschmitt Me 262. This is the miracle jet fighter that has been talked about so much … What I've just seen is unbelievable. The superiority of this fighter is incredible. I wonder why it has only now been put into service. Why so late? It is way too late' (p. 154).

Passing bridges being prepared for demolition, he reaches Schleswig-Jagel airfield, near the Danish border, where a wing of Messerschmitt 262 night-fighter jets is based. They will soon be replaced by a squadron of RAF ground-attack Typhoons. He meets armoured cars of the King's Dragoon Guards as they occupy the area on 6 May 1945. 'The crews huddled inside them don't quite know what to do. They are surrounded by us, and we are still fully armed. The boys from Great Britain attempt to defuse the strange atmosphere with wide smiles' (p. 161).

Karl Knoblauch's war came to an end two days later with the formal surrender in Berlin, which he hears in the Wehrmacht's final communiqué over the wireless.

In mid-January 1945, when adjutant, Knoblauch was asked by his battalion commander, Captain August Wolf, why he kept a diary. His response was enlightening: 'Because I think it's important to record the events we're living through, especially from the point of view of the ordinary man. Works on the history of the war will be published in the future. Everyone will be able to read where and when such and such an army was deployed. But I want to record what happened for men like us and how we conducted ourselves in this extraordinary situation' (p. 77). I hope you, the reader, will agree with me that the author, who died in 2010, achieved this admirably.

Peter Caddick-Adams
Croatia, February 2026

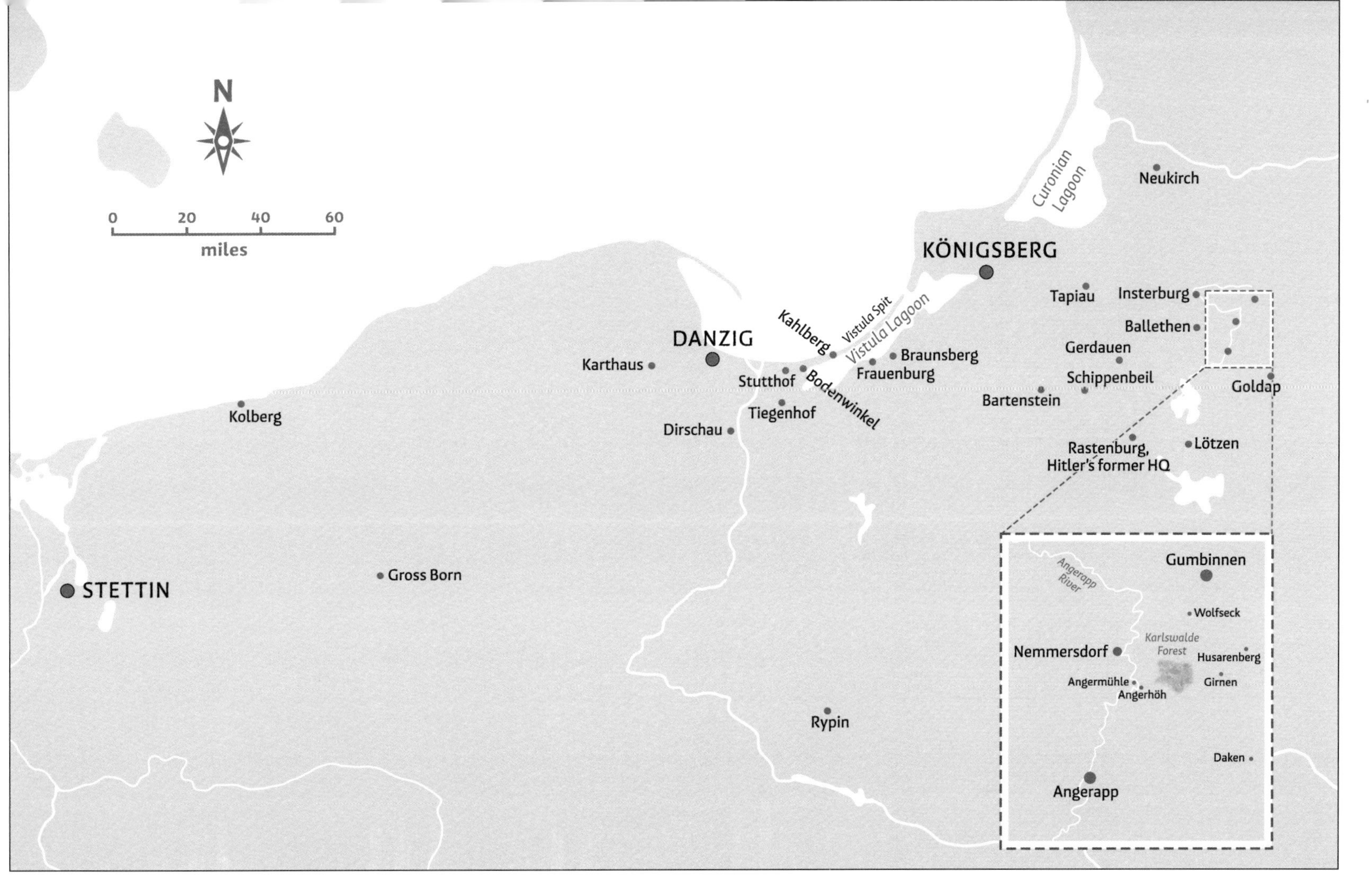

N
0 20 40 60
miles
Curonian Lagoon
Neukirch
KÖNIGSBERG
Tapiau
Insterburg
Ballethen
Gerdauen
Vistula Spit
Kahlberg
Vistula Lagoon
DANZIG
Karthaus
Stutthof
Bodenwinkel
Braunsberg
Frauenburg
Schippenbeil
Bartenstein
Goldap
Kolberg
Dirschau
Tiegenhof
Lötzen
Rastenburg,
Hitler's former HQ
Gross Born
STETTIN
Rypin
Angerapp River
Gumbinnen
Wolfseck
Karlswalde Forest
Nemmersdorf
Husarenberg
Angermühle
Girnen
Angerhöh
Daken
Angerapp

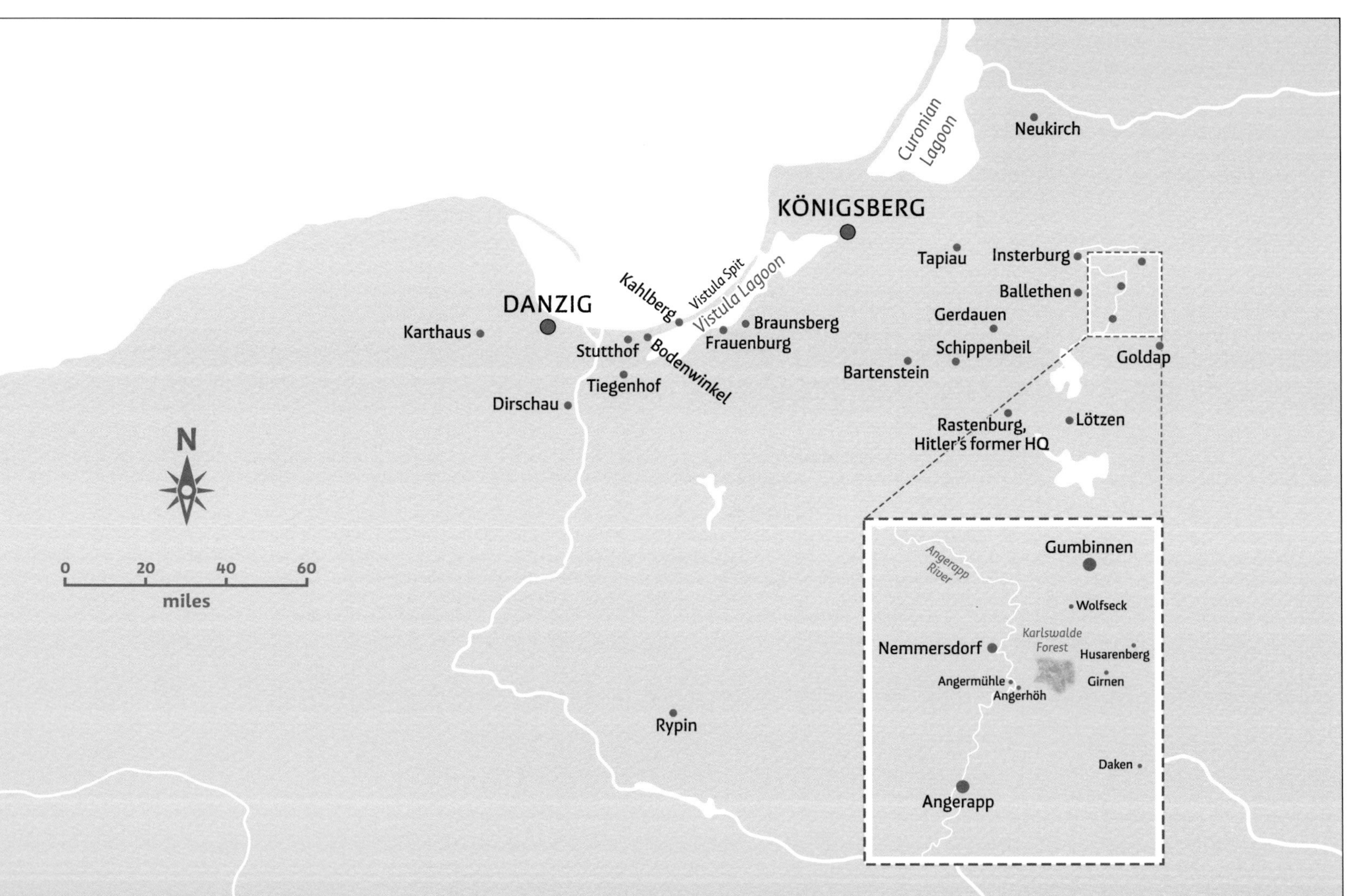

Curonian Lagoon
Neukirch
KÖNIGSBERG
Tapiau
Insterburg
Ballethen
Gerdauen
Schippenbeil
Goldap
Kahlberg
Vistula Spit
Vistula Lagoon
DANZIG
Karthaus
Stutthof
Bodenwinkel
Braunsberg
Frauenburg
Bartenstein
Tiegenhof
Dirschau
Rastenburg, Hitler's former HQ
Lötzen
N
0
20
40
60
miles
Rypin
Angerapp River
Gumbinnen
Wolfseck
Karlswalde Forest
Nemmersdorf
Husarenberg
Angermühle
Girnen
Angerhöh
Daken
Angerapp

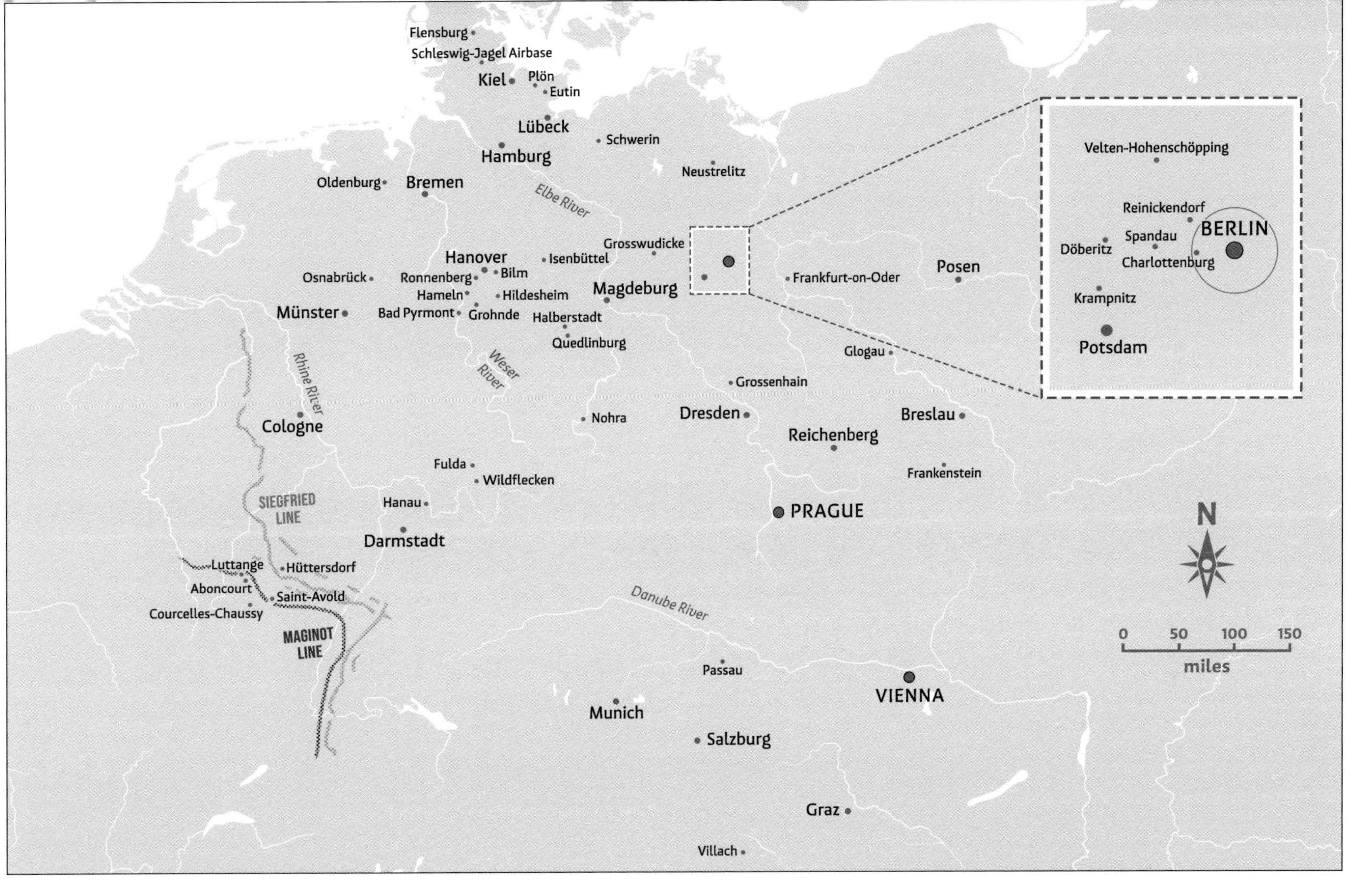

BERLIN
Velten-Hohenschöpping
Reinickendorf
Spandau
Charlottenburg
Döberitz
Krampnitz
Potsdam
N
miles
0 50 100 150
Posen
Frankfurt-on-Oder
Breslau
Frankenstein
Glogau
VIENNA
Grossenhain
Reichenberg
PRAGUE
Graz
Neustrelitz
Grosswudicke
Magdeburg
Dresden
Salzburg
Passau
Villach
Schwerin
Isenbüttel
Nohra
Danube River
Quedlinburg
Elbe River
Halberstadt
Munich
Lübeck
Eutin
Plön
Hildesheim
Kiel
Hamburg
Hanover
Bilm
Schleswig-Jagel Airbase
Ronnenberg
Hameln
Grohnde
Weser River
Wildflecken
Flensburg
Bremen
Bad Pyrmont
Fulda
Oldenburg
Osnabrück
Hanau
Darmstadt
Münster
Rhine River
Cologne
SIEGFRIED LINE
Hüttersdorf
Saint-Avold
Luttange
Aboncourt
Courcelles-Chaussy
MAGINOT LINE

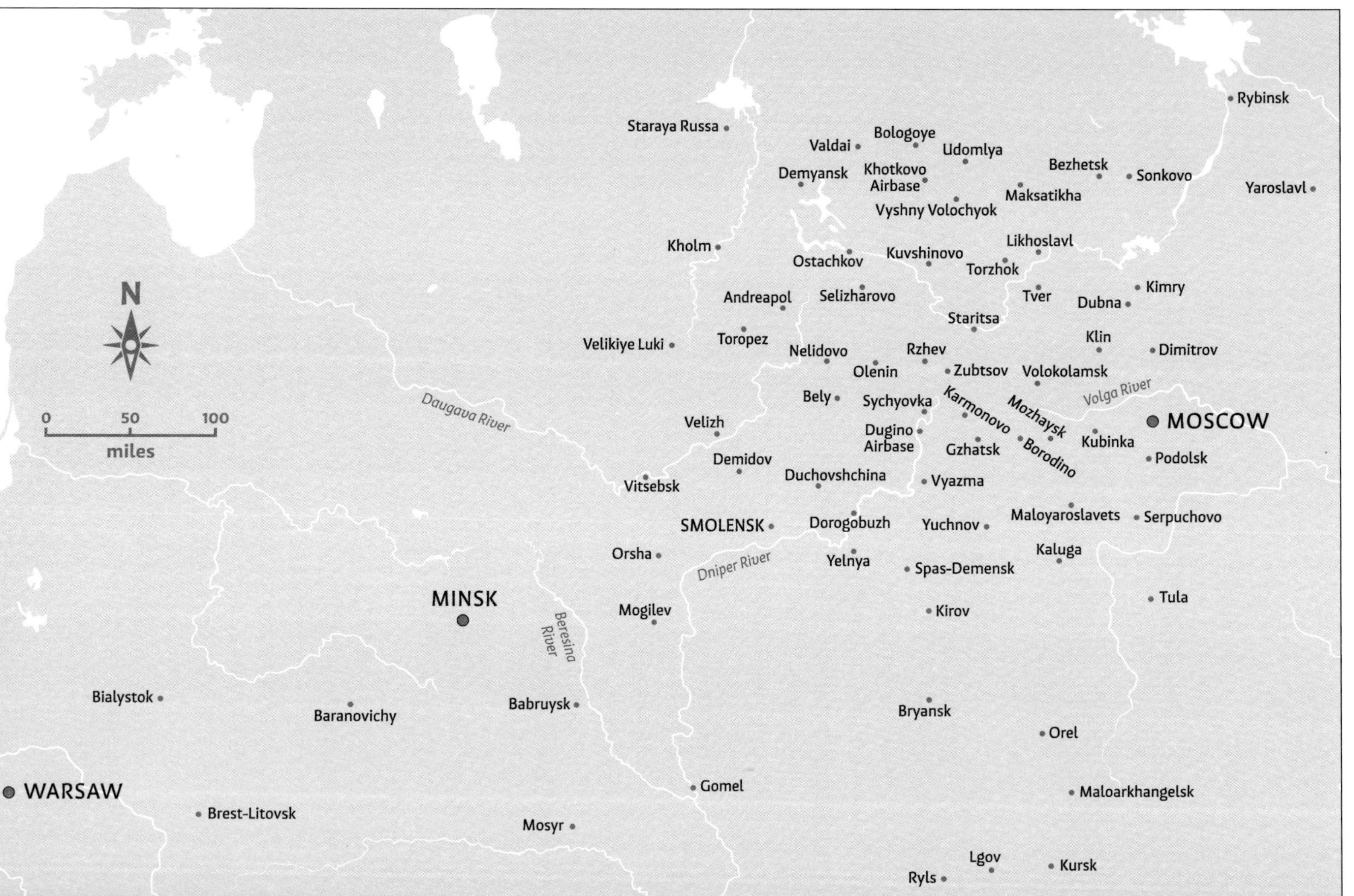

Rybinsk
Staraya Russa
Bologoye
Valdai
Udomlya
Bezhetsk
Sonkovo
Demyansk
Khotkovo
Airbase
Maksatikha
Yaroslavl
Vyshny Volochyok
Kholm
Likhoslavl
Ostachkov
Kuvshinovo
Torzhok
Tver
Dubna
Kimry
Andreapol
Selizharovo
Staritsa
Klin
Velikiye Luki
Toropez
Dimitrov
Nelidovo
Rzhev
Olenin
Zubtsov
Volokolamsk
Volga River
Bely
Sychyovka
Karmonovo
Mozhaysk
MOSCOW
Velizh
Dugino
Airbase
Gzhatsk
Borodino
Kubinka
Podolsk
Demidov
Duchovshchina
Vyazma
Vitsebsk
Maloyaroslavets
Serpuchovo
SMOLENSK
Dorogobuzh
Yuchnov
Kaluga
Orsha
Dniper River
Yelnya
Spas-Demensk
Tula
Mogilev
Kirov
MINSK
Beresina River
Daugava River
Bialystok
Babruysk
Bryansk
Baranovichy
Orel
WARSAW
Gomel
Maloarkhangelsk
Brest-Litovsk
Mosyr
Lgov
Ryls
Kursk
N
0 50 100
miles

Preface

Much has been written about military events, political backgrounds and human behaviours: true and untrue, objective and subjective, and a lot of it is nonsense. Caution is always advised when economic profit is the driving force for the literary depiction of historical events.

My memoirs here are certainly capable of being cast in a dramatic fashion. But I lack any inclination towards drama.

In presenting the events that took place, I am concerned with focusing on the truth and not with modified constructions typical of contemporary historical discourse. And I absolutely do not say anything such as: 'Look at me. I wasn't as naïve as everyone else. I saw it all coming and behaved with restraint!'

My Prussian upbringing will explain some of my conduct that might not be understood today. This applies also to the attitude of my comrades, who like me had been brought up under Prussia's social-aristocratic philosophy of doing much without showing off and being more than you appear to be.

My level-headed record is nothing short of the truth. There are even no pseudonyms whatsoever!

In order not to distort the relationship between the course of events and the mode of behaviour, I have deliberately refrained from inserting knowledge that I only gained after the war.

If the reader forms the view that I have not covered certain topics sufficiently or not covered them at all, this is because such things did not arise in my personal sphere.

I remember with gratitude the comrades who crossed my path in highs and lows and those who walked some of that path with me.

It should also be said that I do not seek recognition for my actions. I only ask that the reader keep an open mind about what I have to say in my account.

Karl Knoblauch
Ronnenberg, 2007

Chronology

Karl Knoblauch's Military Career
Prior to 1944

1940: Participation in the campaign in France as part of the advance detachment of the 95. Infanteriedivision (95th Infantry Division).

October 1941 to September 1943: Operational aerial reconnaissance observer, Luftaufklärung des Heeres Fernaufklärungsstaffel 4.(F)/14 (4th Long-Range Reconnaissance Squadron of the 14th Reconnaissance Group, attached to the army).

2 September 1943: Wounded in air combat against Soviet fighters over Vyazma, (165th combat flight).

THROUGH FIRE AND SKY

Volume II

With the 2nd Parachute Panzer Fusilier Battalion 'Hermann Göring' in East Prussia, 1944–1945

Transfer to Panzerdivision 'Hermann Göring', August–September 1944

From the author's personal records …

1944

August 1944: I am in Bad Pyrmont general hospital and will soon be released. Months of restful convalescence lie behind me.

I arrive at the regional depot for unassigned air personnel in Quedlinburg on the evening of 24 August. I am assigned a room. I have no intention of refurnishing it. I assume my stay will only be temporary.

The depot is an assembly point for aviation personnel. The personnel are given accommodation here after their stay in hospital and reassigned to air units once they're fully recovered.

In the evening, I sit in my room. The inactivity is depressing. I notice that of the large number of pilots, observers, radio operators and aerial gunners that are available for assignment, very few are sent to the front. More and more air personnel are arriving from hospital. The place will soon be bursting at the seams. It seems to me that something is wrong. I decide that I will speak to the commander about my deployment at the earliest opportunity.

7 September: In the morning, I ask the adjutant to arrange an appointment for me with the commander. At 1500 hours, I am standing in front of the gentleman. 'Second Lieutenant Knoblauch reporting as ordered!'

'Take a seat. You asked to see me. What about?'

'Major, after almost a year in hospital, I'm now in a state of health that allows me to be deployed for the service I've been trained. If, Major—'

I don't get any further. The commander stands up and interrupts me with a wave of his hand. 'I've seen from your file that you're no longer eligible for aerial operations, so what is it that you want?'

The commander seems irritated. He stands by the window and looks at me challengingly.

I also stand up as a matter of form. 'Major, I do not assume that my military career has ended with my injury. I think there should be a use for me somewhere other than an air unit.'

The commander becomes more annoyed. 'If you think you have to do something, you can join Panzerdivision "Hermann Göring". I'll leave it up to you to decide.'

He thinks he's brushed me off with that, but now I'm annoyed as well. 'If, Major, you have no other suggestion, then I will go to Panzerdivision "Hermann Göring".'

He narrows his eyes. 'As you wish. Go and see my adjutant. He'll make the arrangements.'

The adjutant, a friendly man, is immediately on top of things. I sign a form and am told that I can expect to be transferred shortly.

On my way back to my room, I wonder whether I've taken the right decision. I'm not sure.

I also wonder why the commander is reluctant to reassign me. If this is his attitude towards everyone, it might explain the large number of bored air personnel here. Of course, there might be other reasons too.

I leave the beautiful Quedlinburg and the inhospitable regional depot for unassigned air personnel on 18 September. My transfer has been settled. I am on the express train to Berlin.

I arrive in Reinickendorf, in north-west Berlin, in the afternoon and report to the Hermann Göring Barracks, which is still a well-kept installation despite the effects of the war.

I am informed at the adjutant's office that I can expect to be with the front-line troops in 14 days at the latest. The division is deployed in the east.

The fighting against the Allied invasion forces is becoming increasingly difficult. The High Command of the Wehrmacht announced on 25 September: 'In western Holland, our troops, in new positions, repelled multiple enemy attacks. In the Arnhem–Nijmegen area, our counter-attacks inflicted further heavy casualties on the enemy forces that had landed from the air, thereby denying them the opportunity to launch a major assault. Local thrusts carried out by the enemy were partially thwarted in bitter close combat. To the west of Arnhem, the remnants of the British 1st Airborne Division fought in a narrow area, and 800 of its men were wounded.' Anyone who listens carefully to this tactfully worded announcement can't fail to notice that our considerable defensive successes haven't prevented significant territorial losses.

Before setting off on my journey to the Eastern Front, I visit my relatives once more in Spandau. I spot that they are in low spirits the moment they opened the front door. My aunt Martha tells me that my cousin Wolfgang, a second lieutenant in the Luftwaffe, was reported missing in southern France some time ago.

I am back in Reinickendorf before nightfall.

On 27 September, the Reichssender [Reich broadcasting company] reports: 'The final resistance of the encircled British 1st Airborne Division was broken in the vicinity of Arnhem on 26 September. In ten days of fighting, the rapidly assembled forces of an SS-panzer corps under the command of SS-General Bittrich succeeded in totally annihilating an elite British division despite the resistance it put up and the reinforcements it received from the air. All attempts by the enemy to relieve the encircled division from the south failed and resulted in heavy casualties. A total of 6,450 prisoners were taken, thousands of dead were identified, and 30 anti-tank guns, other guns, various weapons and 250 motor vehicles were captured. In addition, 1,000 troop-carrying gliders were destroyed or captured, and more than 100 aircraft were shot down.'

I remember my father's words: 'Victory was won – at the price of death.'

30 September: It's time! I've already packed my few belongings. I set off with only my dispatch case and laundry bag.

I am soon standing on the platform at Berlin Zoo Station and waiting for the *Fronturlauberzug* [express train for personnel leaving for the front] to Warsaw. The train arrives and then departs five minutes later.

1 October: The train stops on a stretch of track between Posen and Kutno. We are making slow progress. Hospital trains are travelling in the opposite direction towards Berlin.

In Action with the Parachute Troops,
September–October 1944

We arrive outside Warsaw in the early morning and are ordered to disembark. The wind carries the rumble of artillery fire from the nearby front over to us. The air is trembling.

I am transported northwards by truck to the Modi area and arrive at the headquarters of Panzerdivision 'Hermann Göring'. The divisional combat units are deployed in the combat zone of the IV. SS-Panzerkorps (4th SS-Panzer Corps). The commandant at the headquarters assigns me some accommodation.

2 October: I report to the divisional adjutant, who explains to me and a few other officers who've just arrived that, since we've come from various branches of the Luftwaffe, we will need to be made familiar with infantry combat before being committed to action at the front.

This seems a good idea to me. Among the replacement officers, there are signal communication, flak and air personnel.

We set off a short time later for Rypin, in West Prussia. The town lies between Thorn and Soldau amid sand and heathland. The landscape is very similar in character to that of Altmark.

In the evening we are welcomed by the replacement and training unit in Rypin. The officer in charge of our course of instruction, a captain with severe mobility problems, strongly emphasises the importance of what we are going to learn. I get the impression that most of the 11 of us who are present are voluntarily taking it upon ourselves to serve the Fatherland in a manner which is new to us.

I have a look at the timetable and can see that the subject matter isn't new to me.

We are given fatigues and carbines for combat training. Our chevrons of office remain in our lockers. It somehow feels like the days just after I was recruited, in Frankenstein.

4 October: Our training is going into overdrive. There's no time to lose. Ivan is standing at the borders of the Reich.

On the schedule I can see that advanced combat practice firing, rapid shooting, hip shooting and hand grenade throwing are to be covered. The training is close to the front. Safety regulations are significantly relaxed.

5 October: Machine-gun training takes place in the morning and attack at medium range in the afternoon. Exhausted, in the evening we make our way back to the living quarters.

6 October: We work on attacking and penetrating a trench system. We take it in turns to act as squad leaders.

After we've cleaned our weapons in the evening, the instructor sends for me. 'Leutnant (Pilot Officer) Knoblauch, I observed your actions during training this morning. Have you always been with the Luftwaffe?'

'No, sir. I joined the infantry and took part in the campaign in the West with the 95. Infanteriedivision (95th Infantry Division).'

'Well, that explains things. You're completely out of place here. As a part of the final assessment, I will recommend that you be trained for command of a company.'

With that, I am dismissed.

We leave the camp at 2300 hours and march out to practise night firing. After that, we do night drills.

7 October: We are marching again at 0400 hours. We are utterly exhausted. My lung injury has been affecting my physical performance more than I like to admit.

In the afternoon, before nightfall, reconnaissance patrols are carried out, all by the book. After sunset, the temperature drops significantly.

8 October: I am assigned the role of platoon leader in an attack at medium range. After that it's penetrating and rolling up a trench system. Everything goes quite well.

My fellow officers commit themselves fully to the roles of riflemen, machine-gunners and squad leaders.

Training in combat in woods takes place on the morning of 11 October. In the afternoon, we are made familiar with man-portable anti-tank recoil-less guns and shoulder-mounted anti-tank rocket launchers. After being briefed, we shoot with live ammunition. The effect of the hollow-charge projectiles is enormous.

12 October: According to the timetable, there is to be training in close combat and urban combat. I think it'll be important to get the knack of doing this sort of thing. Anyone who can't manage it will have no chance in an emergency.

Night reconnaissance is on the agenda on 13 October. We eat the last of the food at noon. We are getting hungry by 2100 hours. The lack of rations is waved aside by the instructor with the words: 'Gentlemen, the training here is close to the front. You're just going to have to deal with it!'

The course of instruction comes to an end on 14 October. It has definitely been too short for most of us.

Those of us who participated in the course spend the evening together at the Maiswinkel Inn. Someone has resourcefully acquired some wild ducks which, deliciously prepared by the innkeeper, we savour in good cheer.

We are transported to East Prussia via Strasbourg and Deutsch Eylau on 15 October. We reach Königsberg a day later and then continue at a moderate pace on **17 October** through Labiau and Klemenswalde (near Heinrichswalde). We are now in the elk lowlands to the east of the Curonian Lagoon.

We get off the train in the village of Gross Brittanien. Probably because of the proximity to the front, it looks as if there isn't any more rail traffic. I am given lodgings with the Hellwig family. I admire the calmness of these friendly people. Although the Soviets have already taken Kuckerneese and are therefore standing to the south of the Memel, they are convinced that the German troops will prevent an invasion into Reich territory.

It is about ten kilometres to the front at Kuckerneese. The parachute panzer corps is committed to action there.

If Ivan succeeds in breaking through to the south, the population will be sitting in a mousetrap. No preparations appear to be being made to flee.

18 October: We arrive at the corps and report for duty. The corps commander, Majorgeneral (Brigadier) Schmalz, enters the scene.

After greeting us, the corps commander thinks it appropriate to imply that we ought to have been at the front a long time ago. Such a rebuke certainly couldn't have been expressed more clearly. I do my best to suppress my rising anger.

The adjutant steps forward, picks up a long list and read out the names of the officers and the units they are assigned to. My name is among them. 'Second Lieutenant Knoblauch – corps assault battalion! The commander is here right now. He'll take you with him.'

I go to the other side of the staff quarters and report to the commander of the assault battalion, Oberleutnant (Lieutenant) Lehmann. He greets me with a handshake, has a look at me and then, pointing to the Wound Badge in Silver on my field tunic, asks: 'What's the nature of your wound? Are you impaired in some way?'

'I've gone blind in the left eye.'

Lehmann tells me that, under these circumstances, I cannot be considered for the assault battalion. He goes back to the adjutant with me and explains the situation. The adjutant looks at his list and quickly makes a decision. 'Second Lieutenant Knoblauch, you'll be transferred to the fusilier battalion of 2. Division. To be clear, you'll report to the I Battalion of Fallschirmjägerregiment 16 (1st Battalion of the 16th Parachute Regiment). The commander is Hauptmann (Captain) Teusen. Once the reorganisation of our forces in the area of the 2. Division is complete, the I Battalion of Fallschirmjägerregiment 16 will become the Fallschirm-Panzerfüsilierbataillon 2 "Hermann Göring" (2nd Parachute Panzer Fusilier Battalion "Hermann Göring").'

I find all of this a bit confusing. It feels as if fate has taken matters out of my hands. There is no going back.

It has gone dark. I will be spending the night in Neukirch, 15 kilometres west of Tilsit.

On **19 October**, I arrive with some comrades at divisional headquarters in the lowlands to the east of the Curonian Lagoon.

I notice that everyone is in the process of decamping. A second lieutenant who happens to cross my path explains that the corps is being pulled out of the front and is to be deployed, as he put it, 'somewhere near Gumbinnen'.

I wonder how I am going to find my battalion if all formations are on the march 'somewhere'.

Since I can't spend the winter where I am, I get a lift in a command car that is heading towards Kuckerneese. Perhaps I'll find my battalion on the way.

After just a few kilometres we see vehicles coming towards us. Not knowing what's going on, I ask the driver to stop. I halt one of the approaching trucks and learn that the battalions have been withdrawn from the front and sent to the south. Rearguard units are holding the enemy back.

The deployment of rearguard units means that there is no longer a coherent front line. I jump back into the command car and inform the driver. We drive on carefully.

After another five kilometres we come across a village. There is an oppressive silence among the abandoned houses. We are brought to a halt by a group of parachute troops on the northern outskirts of the village. A sergeant approaches our car. 'Where are you going?'

'I'm looking for Battalion "Teusen" of Regiment 16.'

'No idea where it is,' replies the sergeant, 'but you'll run into Ivan if you continue along here. We're the last ones on this road.'

I get out to have a look round. The noise of battle can be heard to the north of us.

The road we are on climbs gently to the north and then disappears into a depression which can't be seen from where we stand.

'Sergeant, someone's coming from the enemy side,' reports the machine-gun team leader, who has taken up a position with his men in a front garden. We take cover and look along the road to the north. A figure emerges from the dip and comes towards us. They are 200 metres away. They approach very slowly. I watch the machine-gunner as he, as a precaution, checks the iron sights on his weapon.

The sergeant reaches for his binoculars. 'That can't be right. An old woman on crutches!'

Two men rush towards the woman. The others remain in position.

If Ivan attacks now, the situation will become critical. Not only for the old woman but also for the two paratroopers.

We are in luck! The men make it back with the woman a quarter of an hour later.

The woman sits herself down on a bench.

I estimate that she is well over 80 years old. She's exhausted and clings desperately to her crutches.

I speak to her after a short pause. 'Tell me, how is it you're walking around here on your own? Do you have any relatives?'

She answers in an East Prussian dialect: 'No, sir, I don't have any relatives. I left my village yesterday. I'm an old woman and wanted to stay in my home. The Russians won't hurt me, I thought. But then I got scared and fled.'

The sergeant, who's been listening, looks at me and shakes his head.

We can hear an engine coming from the village centre. A sidecar motorcycle stops in front of us shortly afterwards. It's a military police vehicle!

The driver, an Oberfeldwebel (battalion sergeant), gets off the vehicle and comes up to me. 'Second Lieutenant, I've come from Division HQ to find out what the situation is here!'

I stop him with a wave of my hand. 'The parachute troops are fighting the battle here. I'm only here as a guest and am looking for my unit. Talk to the sergeant over there.'

The sound of battle is getting closer. I put the old woman in the sidecar of the military police vehicle. As the engine starts, she takes my hand. 'Many thanks, sir, many thanks!'

The sergeant looks on. 'I hope I don't become as old and helpless as she is!'

'Be careful what you wish for. The chances of growing old here in East Prussia aren't that good.'

There is no reason to stay after that. I still haven't found my battalion.

The driver of the command car, who thinks things are becoming a little dangerous where we are, drives me back. Actually, he wants to go further to the north.

I spend the night at the divisional headquarters. I lie on an old sofa in an abandoned farm worker's apartment.

Although I am tired, I can't sleep. There can be no mistake – the front is getting closer. I don't want to be in a deep sleep if Division decides to withdraw. I might then be rudely woken up by Ivan.

I go outside again shortly before midnight. The night sky to the north keeps flashing brightly. The wind carries the rumble of artillery fire to where I stand.

The night comes to an end. I am up early on 20 October and go to find out what is going on. In the afternoon, I am able to travel by rail in the direction of Insterburg alongside elements of the corps. The distance is less than 50 kilometres.

We make slow progress. It has become dark, and it's recently been getting uncomfortably cold at night.

We travel east through Insterburg on 21 October. From there, it's 25 kilometres to Gumbinnen.

The train comes to a stop at Bernen. I lower the window. The air outside is vibrating. An artillery battle is underway. The rumbling is getting closer and closer. The ground that is being hit by artillery shells is only 600 metres to our north.

The train resumes its journey. I can see wounded men near the railway embankment, retreating to the west. The smell of burning is in the air.

Our train slowly enters Gumbinnen railway station and comes to a halt. Shells from tank guns explode all around us.

The assault guns that have been transported on the stake wagons in front of us roll down the ramps and open fire. We're caught in a deafening inferno. I jump off the train.

A Russian T-34 is burning just 500 metres to the south of the railway line. The units that detrained at the station have gone straight into combat. To the south of Gumbinnen as well as further to the west, roughly in the vicinity of Türen and Angereck, the fire of German 8.8cm anti-aircraft guns can be heard clearly. The units committed to the south and south-west of Gumbinnen are Flak-Abteilung 802 (802nd Flak Battalion), 1./Flakregiment 29 'Hermann Göring' (1st

Company of the 29th Flak Regiment 'Hermann Göring '), I./Flakregiment 5 (18. Flakdivision) (I Battalion of the 5th Flak Regiment (of the 18th Flak Division)) and the Flakregiment 16 (16th Flak Regiment). Also to be heard is the barking of the Soviet tank guns.

I've got myself into such a confusing mess and I still have no idea where my battalion is. What should I do? I decide to head further into Gumbinnen.

I can see the commander of 2. Division 'Hermann Göring' with his first general staff officer and a few motorcyclists in an open space in the town centre in front of a life-sized statue of an elk made of stone or bronze. I don't envy them. How they are planning to regain control of the situation is beyond me. I think it best that I am not seen by the commander.

There is heavy traffic moving along the road in the direction of Insterburg. I'm not sure what I'm supposed to do. It's by no means clear if the Soviet forces that have pushed past to the south will be intercepted or if those of us in the Gumbinnen area will end up being encircled. In fact, I know neither where the front is nor where the rear is.

Convoys of trucks are driving out of Gumbinnen towards Insterburg with remarkable haste. It looks like a retreat! I jump onto one of the last trucks. The driver tells me that the Russians have reached the outskirts of Gumbinnen and crossed the Rominte at Grosswaltersdorf (Walterkehmen) yesterday. He adds to his assessment of the situation: 'My platoon leader says that Ivan has probably already got as far as the Angerapp!'

If that's the case, then it looks like a solid breakthrough. I decide to keep my thoughts to myself.

A village sign appears ahead of us: Krausenbrück! The column comes to a halt. I jump down to enquire about the situation. No one knows what's going on.

I watch the flow of traffic and observe that columns are now going back in the direction of Gumbinnen.

I am convinced that, since they won't move east without orders, this means that the situation can't be as bad as it looks.

I head back towards Gumbinnen on another truck. Soviet artillery shells land near us every now and then. The smell of smoke hangs in the air.

The firing of German anti-aircraft guns can be heard a few kilometres to the south of the Gumbinnen–Insterburg road.

We reach Sodeiken, on the western outskirts of Gumbinnen, after 20 minutes. I get out and, to my great surprise, meet Lieutenant Planert, a fellow participant in the course of instruction in Rypin, who had also been assigned to Fallschirmjägerregiment 16. We agree that we'll search for the regimental headquarters together.

We go into Gumbinnen and come across a captain from our division at the Rominte bridge. I see this as an opportunity to find out finally where our regiment has been deployed.

But here too, we only learn that the regiment is committed 'somewhere south of Gumbinnen'. The captain is unable to give a precise answer as to where the front lies. 'The front is wherever the noise is!' he quips.

So, we'll have to search 'somewhere south'. It's already late afternoon. It will be dark in half an hour. I tell Planert that we'll have to wait until tomorrow to look for the front. Given the unclear situation, it's not entirely out of the question that we'll fall into Ivan's hands. We decide to camp near to where we are. With the last light of day, we head along the arterial road to the south-west on foot.

It has become dark in the meantime. The noise of battle has subsided. The sky to the south-east lights up every now and then due to artillery fire. Shells strike the ground a few hundred metres to our south.

We are alone. We haven't seen a single German soldier in our area. We have no idea where our main battle line lies. Perhaps there isn't one.

I suggest to Planert that we stop where we are. We find an isolated house on the Gumbinnen–Annahof road in which to spend the night. I haven't had anything to eat for ten hours.

I make myself as comfortable as possible in a rickety armchair. I gaze at an empty doorframe. The door itself has been blown inwards by an explosion and is lying on the floor. The windows in the left wall are handing askew on their hinges. The panes are cracked. A light draught flows through the room.

I am startled from my half sleep shortly after midnight by footsteps on the road in front of the house. I reach for my pistol and listen. German or Russian? That's the question.

I can see that Planert is also listening in the darkness. 'What should we do?' he asks quietly.

'Nothing!' I reply, just as quietly. 'We should stay here until sunrise!'

I move carefully towards the door. There is nothing to be seen or heard apart from some flares in the distance above Neuhufen and a shot here and there.

The night passes slowly. I am woken by the morning chill, which has hardly been kept at bay by the door and windows. I glance at the clock. It is 0600 hours on 22 October.

Mist hides the fields. We decide it is time to leave this inhospitable house. While we are considering which way to go, we hear footsteps coming towards us from the direction of Annahof. We jump back into the house. Two figures emerge from the mist. Once they are within 20 metres, I can tell from their helmets that they are paratroopers.

Planert calls to them: 'Hello! What unit are you from?'

The paratroopers are wary. The moment Planert spoke, they moved into the roadside ditch and held their submachine guns at the ready.

We step out into the open again. I address them this time. 'Which regiment are you from?'

'From 16. Regiment, Second Lieutenant!'

'And where is the command post?'

'If you go west from here, you'll cross a railway line. A second one runs 200 metres further to the west. If you go along that line, you'll come across an isolated farmstead after about a kilometre. You'll find Oberstleutnant (Lieutenant Colonel) Schirmer and the regimental headquarters there!'

Planert and I are happy that we finally know where to find the regiment we've been assigned to.

We proceed carefully through the mist and past the few houses to be found in Annahof, cross the railway line, and find the Gumbinnen–Angerapp stretch of track without difficulty.

We can see a farmstead to our right after another 20 minutes.

'That's where the headquarters must be,' Planert says.

And where's the front? Hardly anything can be seen! The mist causes such reduced visibility.

A guard is standing behind a gate pillar at the entrance to the farmstead. He moves forward slowly with his submachine gun at the ready.

'Which way to the regimental headquarters?' I ask.

The guard scrutinises us for a moment and then points to a building at the back of the courtyard. We are received by the adjutant. The commander is asleep, so we have to wait.

The door behind us opens at 0800 hours. An officer stands in the doorway; he looks worn out. I don't know him, but, judging from his appearance, he must be the regimental commander. He wears the Knight's Cross of the Iron Cross.

Planert and I report that we've been transferred to the regiment. Lieutenant Colonel Schirmer greets us with a handshake. 'Welcome to the regiment! Ask the adjutant for the battalions you'll be assigned to. Any questions?'

I have one: 'Apart from our 7.65mm pistols, Lieutenant Colonel, we are unarmed. Where can we get some submachine guns?'

Schirmer looks at me in amusement. 'You seem to be quite new to this business. If, as I understand it, you want to be better armed, you'll need to look around outside. You'll certainly find a useful weapon among the fallen. Anyone who doesn't help themselves around here won't grow old!'

The commander shakes our hands again. With that, we are dismissed.

Planert and I glance at one another. Perhaps we haven't come across as particularly ingenious. So, this was what things are like with the parachute troops. Hell and damnation!

In the Border Battle at Goldap, East Prussia, October 1944–January 1945

The adjutant informs me that I'll find the I Battalion on the southern outskirts of Gumbinnen, near the railway line to Grosswaltersdorf (Walterkehmen).

'If nothing's happened during the night,' he says, 'you'll find the battalion commander, Captain Teusen, at an underpass below the railway embankment!'

Planert's destination is Annahof, so we'll be following the same route. We go back along the railway line to the north. The vast areas to the south of Gumbinnen are still covered in mist. The sunlight isn't able to penetrate it.

There's a Soviet tank a few hundred metres to our east, but we can't see it easily. Its gun fires every few minutes, the rounds flying past over our heads. Bursts of machine-gun fire zip by every now and then and strike the ballast of the railway embankment.

The sunlight gets stronger. The mist begins to dissipate. Infantry fire from the enemy side increases in frequency. We crouch down and stay in the cover of the railway embankment. There is no sign of a German front.

I say goodbye to Planert outside Annahof and come across a group of paratroopers at the road and rail intersection to the south-west of Gumbinnen.

A bleary-eyed rifleman speaks to me from a foxhole. 'Second Lieutenant, what are you doing here?'

I pause and then realise that it's Obergefreiter (Corporal) Reitz, who a year and a half ago was a mess orderly with the 4.(F)/14 (4th Long-Range Reconnaissance Squadron of the 14th Reconnaissance Group). This is the last place I expected to see him.

'Is that you, Reitz? How are you?'

'Good, sir! I like it better here than in mess service with the 4.(F)/14. I couldn't become a pilot, so I just joined the parachute troops. We're all great buddies here!'

'Reitz, you must be able to tell me the location of the I Battalion of Schirmer's regiment!'

'That's us here. There's Second Lieutenant von Majer over there in the roadside ditch. He'll be able to tell you what's going on here.'

Infantry fire flares up. I take cover in the ditch and go to Second Lieutenant von Majer. I inform him of my transfer and ask for the commander.

'Captain Teusen is with a few men over there by the railway embankment and blocking the underpass. You'll be able to get to him so long as it's misty.'

I think about this, then jump out of cover and move towards the underpass. The distance is 500 metres.

I'm in luck. After a few minutes, I reach Captain Teusen and his men. I report my assignment to the battalion to him.

Teusen also wears the Knight's Cross. I wonder whether there are any officers around here who haven't been awarded it. He greets me and remarks: 'Go back to Second Lieutenant von Majer and place yourself at his disposal. If the situation permits, we will discuss your employment this evening.'

With that, I am dismissed.

It's still misty, and I make it back to Group Majer without difficulty.

Majer is in command of the remnants of the 2nd Company. I learn that the company, in conjunction with a flak combat section, repelled massive tank assaults the day before to the south of Wolfseck. Casualties on our side were considerable. The Russians lost several T-43 Stalin tanks. The flak combat section was wiped out.

Second Lieutenant von Majer explains to me that he intends to move his combat group, which still consists of 35 men, further forward under the cover of the mist.

Majer stands up and calls out to the men around him: 'Forward march!'

Utterly exhausted, the men get to their feet and move off in a line, parallel to the railway embankment, to the south.

The mist is noticeably lighter after about 50 metres, and a gust of wind clears away the rest. Open terrain lies to the east. A small wood can be seen ahead on the left. Suddenly there's infantry fire. We start to run.

Now we've been noticed by the enemy tank crews over there. The first shells hit the stretch of track 30 metres in front of us. And then it comes thick as hell. There are explosions all around us in quick succession.

When there's a brief cessation of fire, Majer orders the group to fall back to its original position.

I lie in the roadside ditch and gasp for air. My lung injury is giving me trouble. Three men are dead, amongst them Corporal Reitz. I'm finding it hard to conceal my shock.

At midday Captain Teusen returns with his men. I estimate the strength of the battalion to be about 100 men. I don't know how many officers the battalion still has. I've only met Teusen and Majer.

I can't keep track of the reorganisation of our formations. Majer explains to me that Fallschirmjägerregiment 16 doesn't actually exist any more. It was redesignated

Fallschirm-Panzergrenadierregiment 3 (3rd Parachute Panzer Grenadier Regiment) 'Hermann Göring' some time ago and placed under the command of Panzerkorps (Panzer Corps) 'Hermann Göring'.

At nightfall, Majer sends a small detail along the railway embankment to recover those who have fallen.

The men return with their sorrowful burden half an hour later. Reitz has shell fragments in his head and hip. Another fragment shattered the grip of his pistol. So severe were his injuries that he probably died instantly. I take possession of his helmet and submachine gun.

Second Lieutenant von Majer orders that the dead be buried. By the end of the day, there are three graves to the south-west of Gumbinnen, where the Gumbinnen–Grosswaltersdorf and Gumbinnen–Angerapp railway lines converged, and one of those graves belongs to Corporal Reitz.

At 2200 hours a messenger arrives and informs Majer and me that we are summoned to Annahof for an operational briefing.

We meet a group of officers behind a single-family house.

Majer and I are the last to arrive. I recognise Captain Teusen in the dark, but I don't know any of the other officers.

The briefing is conducted by a major. 'Gentlemen, the spearhead of the 11. Gardearmee (11th Guards Army) has pressed ahead to Nemmersdorf (on the Angerapp) via Grosswaltersdorf (Walterkehmen) and Tellrode (Tellitzkehmen). In the south, Russian tank formations have crossed Reichsstrasse [Reich highway] 132 to the north of Lake Goldap and have pushed further to the west. Our intention is to cut off and annihilate the Soviet formations by executing a pincer operation from the north and south. Panzerkorps "Hermann Göring" will attack in conjunction with the 5. Panzerdivision from the area to the south of Gumbinnen in the direction of the Plicken Hills and Grosswaltersdorf. The Führer-Grenadierbrigade of Panzergrenadierdivision "Grossdeutschland" will strike to the north from Goldap. If our attack wedges are successfully united, the front to the east towards the Rominte will be secure. The advance will begin tomorrow at 06.45!'

The units and formations involved in the operation each receive their own specific orders. Battalion 'Teusen' will initially advance on Wolfseck with the support of assault guns. Further orders will be issued as the situation develops. The main objective is Grosswaltersdorf.

Majer and I returned to the position in the roadside ditch to the south-west of Annahof.

Majer summons the squad leaders and informs them of the planned attack. The men listen with stoic calm. Everyone knows that more comrades will fall in action tomorrow.

I check the sentry posts one more time before settling myself into the ditch. Flares hang in the sky above Keilen and Neuhufen. Shots ring out here and there.

23 October: The night is relatively quiet. I can't sleep. Whenever I doze off for a bit, the cold night air wakes me up.

It's 0600 hours. The man next to me is checking the bolt mechanism of his submachine gun.

Second Lieutenant von Majer is soon on his feet. He waves me over and tells me that I am to assume command of the right group of his battered company. 'Maintain contact with me and see to it that your men stick to the line of advance!' he says.

The men around me seem calm. No one wants to show their inner feelings. I certainly try to remain composed, difficult as that is.

It gets brighter. The horizon in the east is striped with red and yellow between Schweizertal and Altkrug. I glance out of the shelter. It's still quiet over there where Ivan is.

Low-flying aircraft can be heard from the vicinity of Gumbinnen. They won't be German machines. There are hardly any left.

The noise they make gets louder. 'Low-flying aircraft to the left!' I call out, just in case.

Then there they are. Flying just above the treetops, and with their onboard weaponry firing away, they dart in the direction of Eggenhof.

I straighten up and watch the ground-attack aircraft as they circle. We crouch down again when the onboard cannons open fire and churn up the ground around us. And then it's quiet. Thank goodness no one's been wounded.

German assault guns appear on the western outskirts of Annahof. I count three of them. It's by no means overwhelming, but it's better than nothing.

The steel monstrosities come to a halt a short time later on the road in front of us, their engines still running. We're invited to mount them.

Artillery fire starts abruptly to the south of Gumbinnen at 06.45. The battlefield comes alive.

We roll along the road to the south and then, after about 600 metres, turn left into the open field.

The terrain rises. In front of us lies the village of Wolfseck. Russian artillery fires in our direction. Their shells strike the ground a few hundred metres ahead of us. The assault guns pivot to the right and drive to the south at high speed. We struggle to hold on to the swaying vehicles.

Before us is a road running from the left out of Wolfseck to the west. Infantry fire is getting heavier. The assault guns stop in front of the road and open fire. We jump off and take cover.

I try to maintain contact with the assault guns so that we won't get stuck here.

The men around me watch what I'm doing. They're certainly curious about my activities, I can tell. As far as they're concerned, I'm a newcomer. They don't know what to expect from me when the situation puts me under pressure.

Apart from being the newcomer, I'm burdened with a far more serious flaw, and that's that I'm not a real paratrooper! The men who are lying in the dirt around me are fully aware of their worth, but they want to gain some idea of my value.

I come to within 15 metres of the assault gun on my left. I'm about to signal to its crew when a head emerges from the steel hull. 'We've run out of ammunition! We're going back to reload!'

The three assault guns reverse, turn and disappear in the direction of Annahof. I feel weak at the knees. The corporal next to me was listening. 'Shit!' he says.

The terrain in front of us slopes upwards. It's another 400 metres to 'Flak Hill' (Hill 55.8), which is 500 metres to the south-west of Wolfseck and which we are meant to take. It's become strangely quiet ahead of us. Only here and single shots are fired. There's nothing to our right; the flank is open. We can't tell whether there are any German troops on the other side of the Gumbinnen–Nemmersdorf road. In any case, we can't stay where we are. I stand and call out: 'Forward march!'

Utterly exhausted, the men slowly get up. I'm hoping Ivan won't wake up again anytime soon. Open terrain lies ahead of us. I urge the men to hurry.

To our left, east of Wolfseck, I can hear heavy fighting.

Only a few more metres to the top of the hill. We advance carefully, crouching and with weapons at the ready.

I instruct the men to take cover and crawl forward towards the summit. There are stock fences there. I can see the old German anti-aircraft position a little to the left. There's no sign of Ivan. It's eerily quiet.

I decide that the right wing of Group Majer should move into the anti-aircraft position and secure the area to its south.

On my signal, we rush forward with the aim of occupying the foxholes on the southern side of the position.

Suddenly there's machine-gun fire. I can't make out where the enemy is. The enemy fire is so heavy that I don't dare raise my head. The men to my left have taken cover behind an 8.8cm gun.

I attempt to crawl to the left to get out of the zone of fire. There's semi-automatic fire the moment I move. It's probably coming from a sharpshooter.

The man to my right is dead. He lies crumpled on the ground. His gaze is frozen and empty. He died silently.

I lie still for a few minutes. Then I try again to get away. Another shot. Something hits my back. Very carefully, I move my arms and legs. I'm not wounded. A bullet has torn open the rolled-up half-shelter that I'm carrying on my back.

The minutes pass. Sweat drips off my forehead. To my left, I hear someone shouting: 'Over here, Second Lieutenant! We've cut through the fence!'

I look slightly to the left and see the gap in the fence.

If Ivan is at the ready and has me in his sights, he'll get me the moment I jump up. I struggle to decide what to do. Then I can hear noises of battle again. I rush forwards, dive through the gap in the fence and roll for cover. It worked.

I lie in a foxhole and try to calm myself. I'm thinking about my next move when I am shaken by a tremendous explosion. My ears ring.

I carefully peer over the top of the foxhole and see the rocking of the nearby 8.8cm gun. Smoke rises from the end of the barrel.

Only then do I realise what has happened. Three of my men fired on Ivan with the anti-aircraft gun. Even though the sighting mechanism has been destroyed, they simply aimed by looking over the top edge of the barrel.

I look around at the anti-aircraft position. One of the guns has been so severely damaged in the fighting on 21 October that the barrel is hanging askew in its cradle.

Those who died in that fighting are still at their guns. They fought until the very end.

A second lieutenant is slumped in the gun pointer's seat of the 2cm anti-aircraft gun. He was killed by fragments from a tank shell. His lower abdomen is ripped open. I have to look away.

A decision needs to be made. I don't want to get tied up here. Glancing ahead over the southern slope of Flak Hill, I realise that further progress is impossible at this stage. I decide to assemble the men and fall back to Wolfseck so that we can establish contact with the left wing of the battalion.

I call out to the men. We dart out of the anti-aircraft position and into the cover provided by the backslope.

A brief look around brings us to the tragic realisation that four men have been killed in action. Those who have been wounded are carried away in the direction of Gumbinnen.

We go back in single file to the southern outskirts of Wolfseck and then forward again on the road to the south-east.

I meet Captain Teusen and the small number of men of his staff at a barn to the left of the road. I give my report.

The commander explains to me that the remnants of the battalion will assemble where we are. The situation is unclear. As soon as it is dark, the battalion will take up a position between the Wolfseck–Kleinweiler and Annahof–Eggenhof roads at a point approximately 300 metres to the south of Flak Hill.

As to what progress has been made by the other formations of Panzerkorps 'Hermann Göring' and by those of the 5. Panzerdivision, nothing is known. However, I do learn that the town of Golcap has been taken by the Russians.

A lieutenant whose name I don't know says that the Red Army soldiers who entered Reich territory on 21 October massacred the civilian populations in the villages of Nemmersdorf and Schulzenwalde. Many women were raped and then brutally murdered along with children.

In the late afternoon, with the last light of day, we set up a security line to the south of Flak Hill.

The men are physically exhausted. Some of them fall asleep right away. With some effort, I get the others to dig makeshift foxholes. I dig as well. I'm really hoping we'll be pulled out before sunrise.

At 0200 hours on 24 October, a corporal and I walk along the weakly occupied line and come across two of my men. They've fallen asleep at their posts. One of them doesn't even wake when I tap his foot.

Such behaviour would have previously resulted in disciplinary action. By now, however, it's no longer possible to enforce discipline. The men have been worn out for months on end.

I finally get the man to wake up. He groans. 'I can't go on any longer, sir!'

Although it's dark, I can see that the man is trembling in every limb. I try to settle him by appealing to his sense of responsibility. 'Your comrades can't go on any longer either. You need to pull yourself together if you want to survive. You're lucky that it was me that woke you up and not Ivan. Your nap would have turned into permanent sleep!'

The man stands sluggishly. 'Are you going to report me, Second Lieutenant?' His mouth hangs open.

Now I lose it. 'What do you take me for? I told you what I thought and am now expecting that the company can rely on you! I've forgotten all about your nap!'

I leave him and go on with the corporal. We carefully approach the Annahof–Eggenhof road and, after 200 metres, reach a machine-gun emplacement in the roadside ditch which belonged to the neighbouring unit on the right.

We exchange our observations, and I explain to the grenadier troops where our right wing is to be found. After all, the boundary position here is 200 metres wide and not at all covered.

By 03.10, a fire has been smouldering 300 metres in front of us for half an hour. Sometimes it's bright and sometimes it's less so, depending on how the wind is blowing into the embers, but it troubles me. I want to know what's going on and call three of my men over.

Step by step, each of us with finger on trigger, we walk towards the fire. Thirty metres to go, and we are hit with an awful smell.

We finally reach the embers. I scan the area to make sure there's no enemy presence and then examine the ground around the fire as far as is possible in the darkness.

A dead Russian lies there with his feet in the embers. He is slowly roasting. The smell of burning flesh is revolting.

We pull him out of the fire and bury the embers with dirt.

Shortly after 0600 hours, we receive an order that has been passed on from man to man. 'Assemble to the left!'

The men stand up, utterly exhausted as ever. We go back in a line to the southern outskirts of Wolfseck.

The remnants of the battalion assemble at the fork in the road at Point 49.7, approximately 500 metres to the south-east of Wolfseck.

In the meantime the sun has risen. The fields are covered in a light mist. The cool morning air makes me shiver.

The noise of battle can be heard to the south. The battalion marches in a line, considerably spread out, along the road towards Kleinweiler. I am with my group, close to the end of the line.

We have no idea whether there were any other German troops on the move, be it to our right on the Eggenhof–Wilken road or to our left near Samfelde.

We soon reach the wooded high ground of the Plicken Hills via Kleinweiler. The spearhead has come into contact with the enemy. To the south-east, not too far away, the rapid firing of tank guns can be heard.

Ivan disengages, and we set off in pursuit. We leave the Plicken Hills behind and march further to the south.

The roofs of Brauersdorf appear in front of us. Fires are still burning in the rubble of some of the houses. The spearhead of the battalion turns in the direction of Alt Wusterwitz. There are two kilometres of open terrain.

We are in luck and enter the village without any contact with the enemy. There's nothing more than a homestead on the right side of the road. A horrible smell becomes noticeable as we get closer. It's a mix of charred wood and burned flesh.

The advance party fights off the Russian rearguard, after which we keep going. At the exit of the village of Alt Wusterwitz, I spot the wide tracks of tanks on the dirt road. They are made by T-34s! The churned earth is still quite fresh.

Our situation will become critical if we are to be attacked by tanks. The battalion doesn't have any armour-piercing weaponry.

If Ivan, despite his superiority in armour, is retreating from such poorly armed troops as us, it can only mean that the pincer movement from Gumbinnen to Grosswaltersdorf and from Goldap to the north has been successful.

The enemy is retreating so quickly, it's as if he's trying to save his own neck.

The battalion advances further to the south. We reach Erlengrund (Maygunischken) after about an hour. Even here, there's the abominable stink of fire and decay.

A dead Russian has been rolled into the road surface at the village exit. The retreating vehicles of his fleeing compatriots have bulldozed him into the ground. I made sure not to tread on the surface. The stench is overwhelming.

At 1800 hours, by which time it has already become dark, Schwarzenau (Jodzen) is in front of us. We take up a position to the south of the village with the front facing towards Rominte.

The headquarters have been set up in an isolated farmstead to the south-west of Schwarzenau. The commander sends for me. It's the first time that Captain Teusen has found a moment to talk to me about my further deployment. 'Second Lieutenant Knoblauch, please report briefly on your military career – units, deployments, and so on!'

I succinctly outline my career. The commander doesn't interrupt me. When I'm done, he says: 'It's good you're more than just an airman. Tomorrow, if nothing comes up in the meantime, you will take command of the Jäger-Pionierzug (rifle pioneer platoon) of the 4th Company!'

We drink red wine from metal cups. This marks the beginning of my new role.

The men from the companies arrive one by one. The battalion has now set up a line of obstacles between Daken (Dakehnen) and Schwarzenau (Jodzen).

After the heavy casualties of the previous few weeks, the main line of resistance is only very lightly occupied.

25 October: I go outside shortly after midnight and listen carefully in the darkness. It's relatively quiet before the front of the battalion. Flares rise every now and then into the pitch-black night sky above Daken. To the south, perhaps near Goldap, the horizon lights up as if from a distant thunderstorm.

I take command of the rifle pioneer platoon in the early afternoon, or rather the remnants of the platoon. I introduce myself to the men. There is nothing to be done for the time being. The pioneer platoon is the reserve unit at the disposal of the battalion commander.

26 October: Soviet artillery is conducting range-finding fire on our positions.

A messenger from the 2nd Company stumbles through the door at 1500 hours. 'Sir! Lieutenant von Majer has suffered injuries to his eyes! He can't see!'

Captain Teusen stands up. 'Second Lieutenant Knoblauch, you will assume command of the company. The messenger will take you there and bring Majer back.'

I put on my belt, grab my helmet, and go out of the door.

The messenger leads the way. We walk towards Schwarzenau along the roadside ditch. Machine-gun fire forces us to take cover from time to time.

Second Lieutenant von Majer has set up his command post in one of the houses on the eastern side of the village road. We go down the narrow stairs into the cellar. Majer is hunched on a tattered armchair. In front of him is a table with a burning wax candle. He hears us coming and recognises my voice. 'As you've heard, Knoblauch, I can no longer see, but it's reassuring for me that it's you who will take command of this company I care very much for.'

With his eyes closed, Majer points to the map. It shows the company's position. The command post stands on the left wing, and the front runs along the Daken–Schwarzenau road to the south-east.

The five men sitting on old mattresses in the cellar are the only reserve at the disposal of the company.

I thank Majer for the briefing, and then he leaves. The messenger will take him back to the battalion command post.

I now face my new responsibilities on my own. It has become dark in the meantime. The Soviet artillery are subjecting Schwarzenau to continuous fire. The noise is that of a raging inferno. The neighbouring buildings are in flames. Smoke billows into the air.

I go outside with one of my men. We are surrounded by a raging fire. The strong glow of the flames is blinding. It is difficult to see. Chickens and turkeys sit on a wrought-iron lattice either side of a flight of stairs that leads down to the courtyard. They are so frightened that they can no longer move. You could pick them off the lattice like ripe fruit. They have no way of making sense of a world that is falling to pieces.

We visit the company's positions. The foxholes are a long way apart from one another. There is no continuous trench. We can hear infantry fire to the north-east, near Jockeln.

I am in the cellar of my command post again at 1900 hours. I look at the map and consider what to do if Ivan was to attack.

I hear footsteps on the cellar staircase. A messenger appears and asks, 'Are you the commander of the 2nd Company?'

'I am. What is it?'

'Second Lieutenant, the battalion will launch an attack tonight. Here is the written order from the battalion.'

By the light of the candle, I read: 'The battalion will leave its current positions at 0100 hours on 27 October and will assemble 500 metres further to the east in readiness to attack. The attack will take place before sunrise with the support of assault guns. The battalion will wait for the arrival of the assault guns. The objective is to cross Reichsstrasse 132 and gain control of the Rominte.'

I call for one of my messengers and go with him to the foxholes to inform the men and prepare them for the attack.

I return to the cellar in Schwarzenau shortly before midnight.

27 October: A few minutes before 0100 hours, I go outside with the men of the company headquarters. It takes a moment for my eyes to adjust to the darkness.

We go from foxhole to foxhole and assemble the remnants of the company.

As a security measure, two of my men feel their way forward 30 metres in front of us. We follow behind to the left and right with weapons at the ready.

We see flares rising into the sky above the highway, which lies 300 metres ahead. Ivan is there.

Something is happening in the darkness ahead of us. We had hoped that Ivan wouldn't be attacking. I order the company to halt and take cover. I move forward carefully, step by step, and come across one of the two men who had gone on ahead. He grabs my arm and points into the darkness.

We wait a few minutes. I can faintly hear words being spoken in German. There seems to be some sort of mess-up ahead. Are these our own troops, or are they the bastards of the National Committee for a Free Germany, those who have made themselves available to the Soviets and whose activities have already cost the lives of many comrades?

I hear footsteps, almost muffled by the soft soil, coming towards us.

I kneel on the ground. The soldier next to me does the same. Our weapons are held at the ready. Nothing can be seen yet.

The steps come closer. I can't wait any longer. 'Halt! Who goes there?'

'Don't shoot! Germans!' comes the answer.

Three figures approach us through the darkness. I am suspicious and keep my finger on the trigger.

A sergeant and two men from the neighbouring company appear before me. I identify myself and learn from them that the assembly of the battalion on this unusually dark night hasn't got anywhere. The companies are in disarray. It is a good thing we didn't start shooting at one another.

The sergeant has been given the task of recalling the companies to their old positions near Schwarzenau. This is no enviable task.

I go to my men and lead them back to Schwarzenau. They occupy their old foxholes again, and I go into the cellar command post with the company headquarters personnel.

The nervous tension has subsided by 02.50. I realise how tired I am.

I hear voices coming from the cellar entrance, and soon the divisional first general staff officer is standing in front of me. I start to deliver my report, but Major Schweim stops me with a wave of his hand and sits on a box. He points to the map on the table and says: 'Tell me, how could this confusion with the assembly of the troops have happened?'

'I don't know, Major. I didn't even reach the jumping-off position for the attack.'

'Well, be that as it may,' continues the major, 'the whole thing will be repeated. You will be at the jumping-off position at 0400 hours. Everything else will remain as ordered. Any questions?'

'No, Major!'

The general staff officer stands, salutes, and goes up the cellar staircase. We are alone once more. The leader of the company headquarters personnel speaks: 'Who was that major, Second Lieutenant?'

'That was Major Schweim, the first general staff officer of our division. If he's personally seeing to the preparations here at the front, you can be sure that the corps attaches great importance to our actions.'

We reach for our weapons at 03.10. I put out the candle, and we ascend the cellar staircase.

We do everything as before. I gather my men, and we carefully proceed in a line towards Reichsstrasse 132. The terrain slopes downwards to the east to begin with. I lead the way to ensure that we stick to the correct direction for our march.

We come across a small cemetery 500 metres to the north of Daken shortly before 0400 hours. There is a Panther there that has been put out of action. On the other side of the road, not far from an intersection, is an inn. The road itself leads to Tollmingen (Tollmingkehmen) via Langenwasser (Langkischken).

I beckon the leader of the company headquarters personnel over to me. 'We'll set up the command post here, behind this Panther. Have some foxholes dug. Keep in mind that we might be spotted after sunrise. Ivan is in the ditch beside the Reichsstrasse and in the inn on the other side of it. I'll brief the company now.'

The company follows me in a line. We go down into a depression which runs northwards from the cemetery. I assign the men their positions and order them to dig in. The terrain before the company's front rises markedly towards the east in the direction of the highway. I hope that the attack will begin as planned before sunrise. If that doesn't happen, we'll be sitting ducks. I can't bear to think of the consequences.

I remind the men to dig in as we make our way back to the command post.

The leader of the company headquarters personnel has been busy in my absence. Although it is dark, I can make out the foxholes that have been dug and I'm grateful for the one that has been prepared for me.

In order to establish contact with the unit on the right, one of my men and I proceed carefully along the rear of the cemetery in the direction of the road. Extreme caution is necessary, as we don't know precisely where Ivan is.

Just before the road, at a point where a narrow path leads to the cemetery, someone calls out to us. I also hear the safety catch of a carbine being flipped. 'Halt! Who goes there?'

'Division "Hermann Göring"!'

We approach slowly and meet the left wing of a battalion belonging to Division 'Grossdeutschland'. We are in distinguished company.

It is a comforting thought to have the formation of a Reich division right next to us.

After exchanging our observations, we talk about the attack that lies ahead. The 'Grossdeutschland' soldiers are confident. I keep my doubts to myself.

The battalion is in its jumping-off position at 0400 hours. It is still dark. Flares are being fired from the highway. Ivan has become suspicious. The firing points reveal to us that we are quite close to his right wing.

I inspect our position again. The men have dug only rather shallow foxholes. I tell them we'll need to dig deeper into the ground.

There is light on the horizon in the east at 06.40. It is ushering in the morning. The air is unpleasantly cold. The grass is covered in dew.

I gaze at Peterstal through the binoculars. All is quiet. There is no noise from the assault guns that are supposed to provide us with cover. There are no flares to signal the commencement of the attack.

It is getting brighter. I look down at the pitiful foxholes in which my men have taken cover. I shiver.

If we are to launch an attack now, we will have to advance across open and rising terrain towards the Reichsstrasse in broad daylight. And we will have no support from heavy weaponry.

If we don't attack, those who couldn't bring themselves to dig deeper into the ground will lie in the line of fire of the Russian guns.

By 07.30, an eerie silence still prevails in the fields between Reichsstrasse 132 and the Daken–Schwarzenau–Peterstal line.

Time passes slowly. It is now fully daylight.

I hear the revving of heavy engines to the north. I reach for my binoculars and gaze through them in the direction of Peterstal. Flares are rising into the sky. The grenadier units have launched an attack. And then I see some assault guns. Far too few!

I struggle to decide whether we should advance. My men will have to cross 200 metres of open terrain, uphill and without the support of heavy weaponry. There will be no chance whatsoever of reaching the road.

First, I wait to see whether the unit to our right will take the inn that lies before us as arranged. That will be the precondition for any activity by my company.

My thoughts are interrupted by a firefight breaking out immediately to our right. The 'Grossdeutschland' grenadier troops have sprung forward.

I have my troops deliver flanking fire with our machine gun on the positions next to the highway to the north of the inn. It becomes lively in the ditch on the opposite side of the road from where we are.

There are explosions from hand grenades and bursts of submachine-gun fire. Then there is a sudden silence. A wounded man calls out for a medic.

I jump out of cover and run behind the cemetery to the road. A burst of machine-gun fire forces me to the ground.

I carefully raise my head. Two dead bodies lie on the road. They've been caught by Russian fire while rushing towards the inn.

The attack by the 'Grossdeutschland' grenadier troops has failed. That means that my company is stuck where it is.

I dash back through the cover of the cemetery and I'm soon with my men.

A glance to the north reveals that the grenadier troops, with the support of the assault guns, have crossed the Reichsstrasse to the east of Peterstal. If the attack maintains its momentum, the Rominte will certainly be reached. I hope that this will lead to the withdrawal of the Soviet units in front of my company.

We are still stuck at 1100 hours. Any movement is out of the question. The men in their feeble foxholes by the highway aren't even able to intervene in the firefight.

Any man who raises his head is immediately fired upon by the Russians from their elevated positions on the road.

I reach for my binoculars. I look from one foxhole to the next. There is no movement down there. I can't tell who is still alive. It is only with the utmost effort that I manage to suppress my agitation.

One of my men speaks: 'I can see the heads of the Russians poking out from the ditch here and there. May I shoot at them?'

I wonder whether this will invite Russian fire against the command post and thereby make it impossible for me to lead the company. If Ivan shells our Panther with his anti-tank guns, we'll have to change our position.

A glance at my men, who are pinned down in their foxholes and whose survival has now become a matter of chance, is the deciding factor. 'You may fire, provided you take care that Ivan doesn't spot any muzzle flashes!'

The man slides under the Panther and takes aim. I look through the binoculars. The shot is fired. The head of one of the Russians goes down and the barrel of his rifle flies up.

Karl Knoblauch as a second lieutenant with the German Cross in Gold on his jacket. He ended his military career in May 1945 as a first lieutenant.

In September 1944, Karl Knoblauch joined Fallschirm-Panzerdivision (Parachute Panzer Division) 'Hermann Göring', in which many Luftwaffe personnel had become engaged in ground combat. Hermann Göring himself wanted to have his own panzer troops.

Josef (Jupp) Reinardy, pictured here in Baranovichy in June 1944, was a pilot who was a good friend of Karl Knoblauch and who flew many missions with him in 1942 and 1943.

Flight Lieutenant Emil Badorrek, commander of the 4.(F)/11 (4th Long-Range Reconnaissance Squadron of the 11th Reconnaissance Group), with Squadron Leader Otolski, the commander of the Fernaufklärungsgeschwader 2 (2nd Long-Range Reconnaissance Wing), in summer 1944.

The graves of Pilot Officer Josef Reinardy, posthumously awarded the Knight's Cross on 24 January 1945, and Squadron Leader Emil Badorrek, commander of the Fernaufklärungsgeschwader 3 (Knight's Cross on 22 November 1943, Oak Leaves on 18 November 1944), who were fatally shot down near Krakow on 26 December 1944 along with Gerd Siller and Franz Felician. Karl Knoblauch was therefore the only one of his old air crew to survive the war.

Visit by the Commander-in-Chief of the Luftwaffe to Fallschirm-Panzerkorps (Parachute Panzer Corps) 'Hermann Göring', Gut Austinshof, November 1944. From left: Reich Marshal Göring, chief of staff Lieutenant Colonel von Baer, orderly officer Second Lieutenant Kleine-Sextro, commander Major General Schmalz, quartermaster Major Grün. Photo: Otte.

Major, later Lieutenant Colonel, Gerhart Schirmer, commander of the Fallschirm-Jägerregiment 16 (16th Parachute Regiment).

Major General Wilhelm Schmalz, commander of Fallschirm-Panzerkorps 'Hermann Göring'.

The once proud Commander-in-Chief of the Luftwaffe is brought back down to earth. In East Prussia in autumn 1944, Major General Schmalz shows him the position of his division on the border with Russia.

Captain Hans Teusen, commander of the I Battalion of the Fallschirm-Jägerregiment 16.

Captain, later Major, Hans von Majer, initially commander of the 2nd Company of the Fallschirm-Jägerregiment 16 and later a battalion commander in the Fallschirm-Jägerregiment 27. His award of the Knight's Cross has not yet been verified, which means that he does not appear in the official list of recipients of the Knight's Cross, but he is regarded by Schirmer and in divisional paratrooper literature as having received it.

First Lieutenant Lehmann, commander of Korpssturmbattaillon (Corps Assault Battalion) 'Hermann Göring', went missing in action in East Prussia in October 1944.

Captain August Wolf, commander of the Fallschirm-Panzerfüsilierbataillon 2 (2nd Parachute Panzer Fusilier Battalion) 'Hermann Göring' from 18 November 1944 until 25 January 1945.

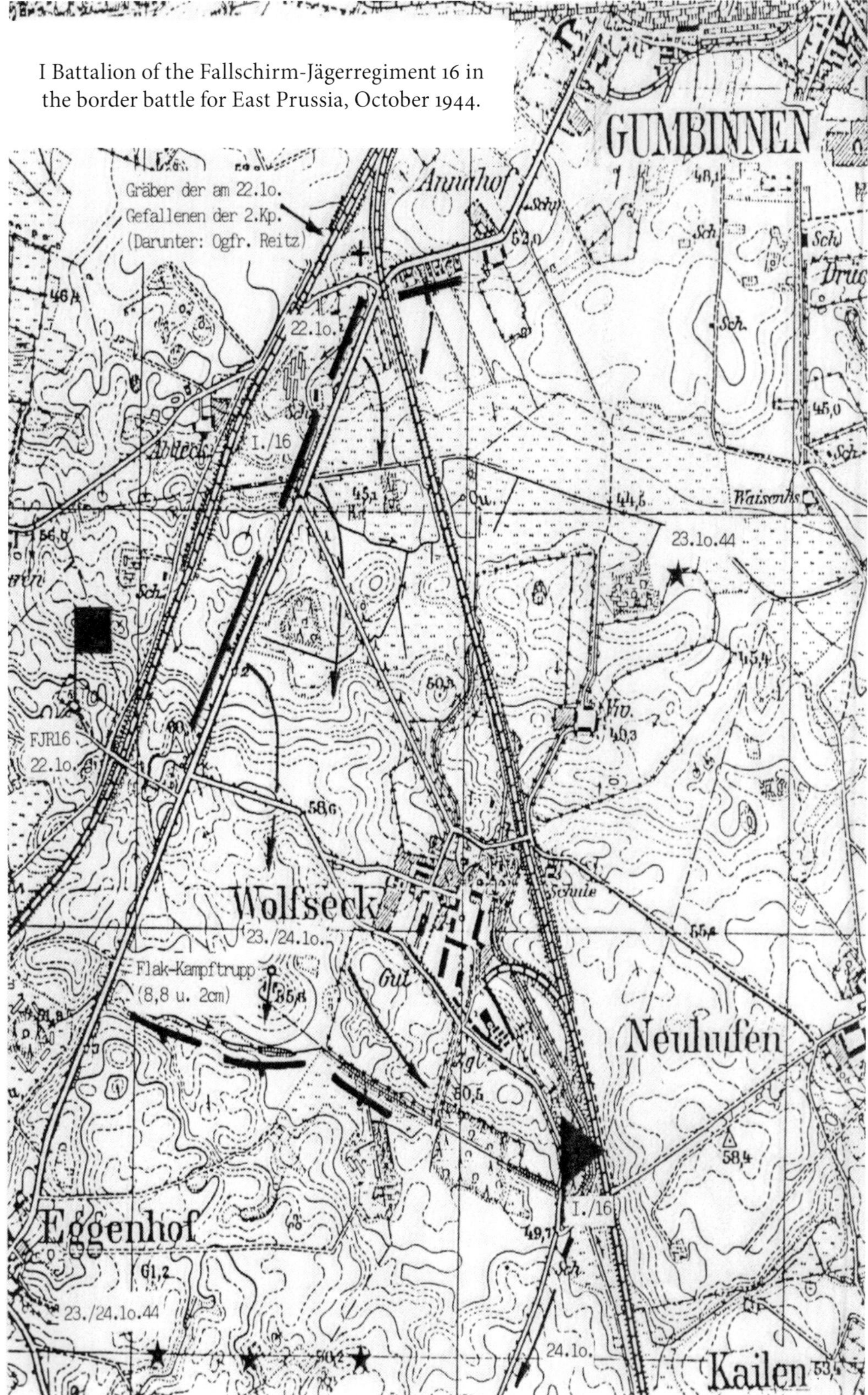

I Battalion of the Fallschirm-Jägerregiment 16 in the border battle for East Prussia, October 1944.

The contested rail and road crossing at Wolfseck, south-east of Gumbinnen, in October 1944.

Counter-attack by the 'Hermann Göring' formations at Weidegrund, north-east of Grosswaltersdorf. The quality of the picture was affected by the chaos of battle.

Two 8.8cm anti-aircraft guns at Wolfseck-Kailen during the border battle for
East Prussia in October 1944.

The contested Gumbinnen–Husarenberg railway line.

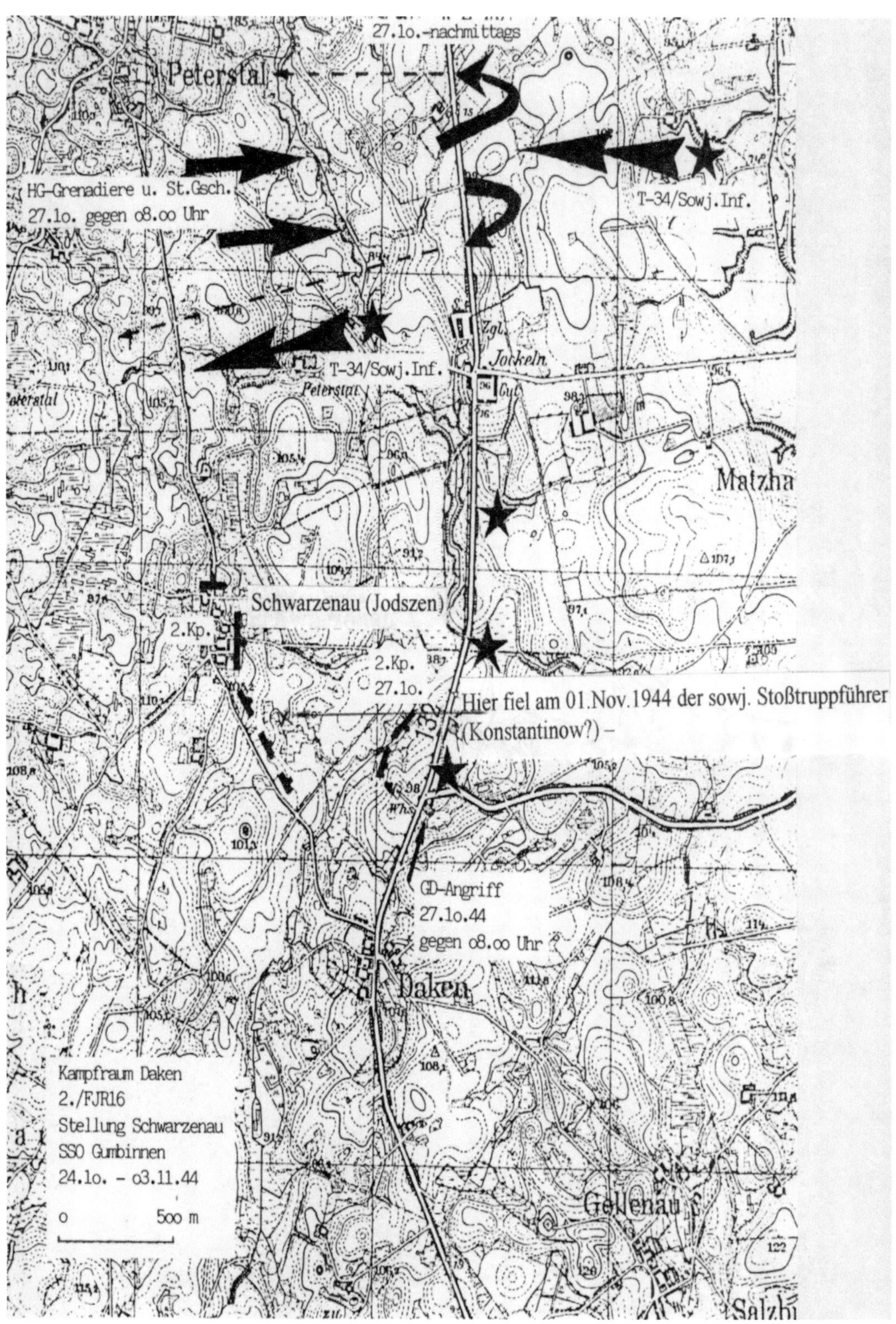

Combat zone in the vicinity of Daken, with the 2nd Company of the Fallschirm-Jägerregiment 16 in the Schwarzenau position to the south-south-east of Gumbinnen, from 24 October to 3 November 1944.

This Russian T-34 tank has been completely torn apart by its own supply of ammunition exploding.

Another T-34 that has been put out of action near Husarenberg and Gertenau, October 1944.

The Soviet 11th Guards Tank Army was stopped in its advance on Nemmersdorf. Unspeakable atrocities were committed by Red Army soldiers against civilians.

An assault gun belonging to a 'Hermann Göring' unit conducting a counter-attack.

One of the many disabled T-34s is being inspected.

The man takes aim again. I have to hold him back. 'Not again so soon, otherwise these buggers will finish us off. Wait a few minutes.'

I notice that his face has taken on a strange expression, one of cold ruthlessness. He can't be more than 19 years old. Before he raises his carbine again, I say: 'Tell me, what's making you so trigger-happy?'

'There's a good reason, Lieutenant!'

'What is it?'

The corporal responded: 'When Ivan pursued us from Ebenrode to Gumbinnen about a week ago and Second Lieutenant Stein was killed, I was taken prisoner along with a few comrades. We had to line up and step forward one by one. My comrades had to kneel and were then shot in the back of the neck. I froze to the spot at first, but then I just ran away. Before the Russians realised what was going on, I'd taken cover where they couldn't shoot at me. I was in luck and made it back to the battalion. That's why, Second Lieutenant, nothing more.' He tries to smile. He doesn't quite manage it.

Another shot rings out. Another Russian slumps into his foxhole.

I looks to the north. I can't believe what I see. The grenadier troops who pressed ahead across the highway in the direction of the Rominte are now retreating. Even the assault guns are moving back towards Peterstal.

A swarm of T-34s are in pursuit. The consequences of the withdrawal of the grenadier units are alarming. I can't see any German troops between Schwarzenau and Peterstal. I wonder what I can do to prevent my left wing being outflanked. I have to get my men out of this terrible situation. But how?

Abandoning the position without orders to do so is impossible. Absolutely unthinkable! I need a decision from the commander, and he is in Schwarzenau.

'I need someone to go to the battalion. Any volunteers?'

A corporal puts his hand up.

I explain his mission to him. 'You need to try to get to the commander in Schwarzenau. Report to him that the company is tied down here and that it will be ground down if it cannot get out. Report also that I request permission to fall back to Schwarzenau. If the commander agrees, three white flares are to be fired. Now jump down the slope here into the depression. Ivan won't be able to see you there. Then try to get to the road to Schwarzenau. If you come under fire, stay down and only get up if you think Ivan's forgotten about you. Have you got all that?'

The corporal goes, with neither helmet nor carbine, down the slope behind us.

He disappears into the depression and reappears after a few minutes on the opposite slope on the road to Schwarzenau. He is about 600 metres from the outskirts of the village. We watch as if spellbound. He's covered 200 metres so far.

Then Ivan stirs. Machine-gun fire lances towards the road. The corporal takes cover. I look through my binoculars. No movement!

'Get the machine gun ready. We'll fire on the highway where Ivan is once our man gets going again.'

Several minutes tick by.

'He's moving again, Second Lieutenant!'

He is indeed moving again. His steps become smaller and his pace slower. He is going uphill.

Ivan has certainly spotted him. The road comes under fire.

We open fire with our own machine gun. The Russians are forced to take cover for a short time. But then an anti-tank gun fires at the corporal. He goes down.

We wait. Two minutes. Five minutes. Ten minutes. I can feel the eyes of my men on me. Each of them expects me to say something. I look through my binoculars. The corporal lies on the side of the road behind a fruit tree whose trunk has been torn to pieces. His position is unnatural. No one who takes cover lies like that. The man is dead.

My men don't need to ask what has happened. They already know that we've lost a comrade.

Half an hour goes by. There is no movement in the company's foxholes.

Something has to be done. I have to make a decision even if it's without the approval of the battalion. But then one of the men speaks to me. He's the one who was taken prisoner by the Russians between Ebenrode and Gumbinnen and who managed to escape and avoid being shot. 'If you agree, I'll do what I can to get through to Schwarzenau.'

I hesitate, but then agree. I wouldn't have given the order myself at that stage.

He also puts down his carbine and helmet and then goes down the backslope. I order that the machine gun is brought into position.

Our man reaches the road on the opposite slope. He doesn't run. He walks and takes cover every 20 metres or whenever he is shot at.

We watch him intently. The Russian fire intensifies, targeting not only our positions but also our man. Another anti-tank gun is in action.

I order that our machine gun open fire on the left flank of the Russian positions.

Our assault guns are engaged in defensive combat against overwhelmingly superior numbers of T-34 tanks in the vicinity of Peterstal.

Our man is on the move again. My hands, holding the binoculars, tremble.

The anti-tank gun fires again. The man is on the ground.

We wait. Two minutes. Four minutes. Fifteen minutes. No movement. My hands are sweating. The men around me gaze at me. I stare into space.

'There!' exclaims one of the men. 'He's on his feet! He's running!'

I call louder than ever to the machine-gunners: 'Fire! Fire!' The machine gun hammers away, spraying fire in the direction of the highway.

I reach for my binoculars again. The man runs, throws himself down, runs some more, and then disappears behind a small hill. He's reached Schwarzenau. We look at one another silently. The corporal next to me utters: 'My, oh my!' Then he turns away. I remove my helmet and wipe the sweat from my forehead.

It is suddenly clear to me at that moment how dire it can be to take command of an unfamiliar company and lead it into action without any opportunity of getting to know the men of the unit. I know hardly any of my soldiers by name. Some of them I haven't even seen before.

Apart from my name, these men don't know anything about their company commander. Yet what is astonishing is that, from their point of view, the second lieutenant is the second lieutenant regardless of what his name is or where he comes from. He is in command and is responsible for the execution of tasks and for the lives of his men. I am impressed by the trust the young soldiers show in me, the unknown second lieutenant.

The relationship between officer and men has evolved in Prussia over the course of more than 200 years. Even the defeat in World War I hasn't brought about an end to the phenomenon that is the frequently invoked and much maligned Prussian spirit, something which is surely not uniquely Prussian.

What induced those two men to voluntarily set off on the difficult and dangerous journey to Schwarzenau?

The first white flare is shot into the sky above Schwarzenau. Shortly afterwards comes the second and then the third. I now have freedom of action. We can fall back to Schwarzenau.

I call one of my men over. 'Go down the backslope until you're within earshot of the first man in the foxholes down there. Stay under cover and inform him that the whole company will fall back to Schwarzenau in one go. We will proceed via the ditch behind us. It will go badly if we try to withdraw up here. Anyone down there will be able to see us. This message is to be passed on to all the men.'

The man grabs his carbine, crawls out from under the Panther, and goes down the backslope. Without difficulty, he gets within calling distance of the right wing of the company.

I look through my binoculars and see that the message has been received. The men stir gingerly. They've been lying there in their foxholes, as good as dead, for hours.

The man returns. 'Order carried out!'

It would be impossible to do anything on the battlefield without men like this! Everyone knows that. I thank him and ask, 'Do you think our comrades down there have understood what we're going to do?'

'I think so, Second Lieutenant!'

Five minutes go by. I speak to the company headquarters personnel. 'It's time! We'll go together into the ditch below. Let's go!'

I am soon on the backslope with the men right behind me. We take cover in the ditch and wait.

I look to the north. Some of the men emerge from the depression. Then there are more, and then finally the rest.

After waiting a few minutes, I ask a non-commissioned officer, 'Do you think the entire company is here now, or is it possible someone hasn't noticed that we're withdrawing?'

'That's impossible. The men who've stayed are already dead!'

In the ditch around me are what is left of the 2nd Company. I count 26 men.

'Listen, everyone! We're going back to Schwarzenau now. In a line. A distance of 20 metres between men. When we're out of cover, it's every man for himself. Let's go!'

The first few men approach the road, which is in fact nothing more than a reasonably good dirt track leading in the direction of Schwarzenau.

The noise of battle can be heard, coming from Daken and Peterstal. We are now in a long line on the slope that can be seen by the Russians from the highway. And then everything starts happening. Rifle fire intensifies, and several machine guns are targeting our withdrawal movement at the same time.

The advance element, which is about 100 metres in front of me, has taken cover. I call out: 'Don't stay there! Keep moving!'

The line ahead gets moving again.

Enemy fire further intensifies. I find I'm getting short of breath. My lung injury was only 13 months ago and is still causing me difficulties. My strength is diminishing. I take cover.

I can't stay there. I jump up and rush on. Some of my men are still behind me.

Then there is anti-tank fire. Ivan is shooting at the trunks of the fruit trees that line the road. Splinters hiss through the air.

I make it another 100 metres. My strength is rapidly dwindling away. I have to take cover.

Someone is on the ground in front of me. I call to him. No answer. Carefully crawling forward on my stomach, I discover he is dead.

I jump up again. With my vision hazy, I stagger across the final 50 metres and finally reach the cover of the last hill. Four men arrive after me.

We approach the houses on the outskirts of Schwarzenau. Captain Teusen comes up to me. I report.

I close my eyes for a moment. I am so physically exhausted that I have to lean against the wall of one of the houses.

The commander informs me of the situation and gives me new orders: 'Despite some initial success to the east of Peterstal, the attack on the Rominte has failed along the entire front. You and your company will secure Schwarzenau and then, after nightfall, you will occupy the old positions south-east from here. Rations and ammunition will arrive once it's dark. Any questions?'

No, I don't have any questions. I certainly don't ask about replacement personnel. Such a thing can't be counted on.

The company still has a combat strength of 24 men. Two fell during the withdrawal. I ask: 'Who is wounded?'

Eleven men raise their hands.

'Do any of you need to leave the company due to your injuries?'

All but one of the raised arms go down. I have a look at the man's wound. A pointed bullet has pierced his upper arm. The bleeding hasn't stopped yet. I send him to the dressing station.

'Listen everyone! We will now occupy the outskirts of Schwarzenau with the front facing east and north. Once it's dark, we will move back into the old foxholes. I will brief each man individually. Both machine guns will cover the north to begin with. The situation between Schwarzenau and Peterstal is not known. Anyone not assigned to guard duty should hit the sack. I can be reached in the cellar of this house. Let's go!'

The men, utterly exhausted, go to their positions. Nothing more needs to be said at that moment. Everyone knows what is necessary.

I go down into the cellar with my company headquarters personnel. It was here, 24 hours ago, that I took over command of the company from Second Lieutenant von Majer. Was that really only 24 hours ago?

Returning to my cellar after inspecting the company's positions, I pick up my diary and in the dim illumination provided by a Hindenburg light I write about the events that took place today.

It is in this moment of relative calm that the full extent of our losses becomes clear to me. Six of my men have been killed in action in the last 24 hours. I dwell grimly on this. Even if only two men fell per day, the 2nd Company would still be annihilated within 12 days! If the situation doesn't change – and it won't change – we'll all be lying dead on East Prussian soil by 8 November at the latest.

I push these gloomy thoughts aside and wonder what the situation is like on the fronts in France and Italy. No news is getting through to us.

It has become dark in the meantime. I hear a vehicle engine outside. I go up the cellar steps and see a command car in the cover of a house wall. A non-commissioned officer jumps out and says casually, 'We've got rations and ammunition for you. It's not much, but there aren't many of you left either!'

I call for one of my men from the cellar. We get the supplies unloaded.

I have a machine gun brought back from the northern outskirts of the village and have the men move into the foxholes south-east of Schwarzenau.

I decide that the machine gun that has been brought back should be positioned on the right wing. If Ivan conducts a frontal assault on the village, his flank will be caught in our machine-gun fire.

It is remarkably quiet in front of our position. I think I'll try to get some sleep. My men will be able to wake me if anything happens outside.

It is pitch-black at 2100 hours. I inspect the position. The men in the foxholes haven't made any noteworthy observations in the sloping terrain.

There are two men in each foxhole. One sleeps, the other stays awake. The distance from one foxhole to the next is more than 50 metres. Infiltration by the Russians can't be ruled out in this darkness. We'll have to be on our guard.

28 October: The night is over. Nothing has happened. Perhaps Ivan has enough to deal with of his own.

Artillery fire on Schwarzenau commences at 1000 hours. Bits of plaster fall from the ceiling of our cellar.

Once there is a break in the fire, I go outside and inspect our position in the open terrain. The foxholes have been subjected to mortar fire. The firing of an anti-tank gun can be heard every now and then. There is no sign of the men who had manned the position. I return to my cellar.

It is beginning to grow dusk outside. I get ready to go and inspect the positions. I hear footsteps on the cellar stairs. A corporal stands in the doorway. 'Second Lieutenant, the machine gun on the right wing was put out of action ten minutes ago! There was a direct hit on the machine-gun emplacement. The crew are dead!'

Accompanied by the corporal and some of my men, I go to see the positions. The foxhole with the machine gun is a terrible sight. This direct hit is a fluke for the enemy, but it doesn't make it any less dreadful.

Both soldiers have been ripped apart beyond recognition. Our efforts to find their identification tags are unsuccessful. I have them placed in tarpaulin, call the double sentry to the left over to me, and arrange for the transport of our dead comrades back to Schwarzenau. Everything has to be done as quickly as possible, for the exposure of the right wing of what was already a very weak position cannot be allowed to last for too long. But I believe that I owe this service to the fallen. I think of the dead comrades who still lie in the foxholes near the highway and of those who didn't survive the withdrawal to Schwarzenau. They won't be able to be recovered. Who will bury them? When and under what circumstances will this happen?

More artillery fire on Schwarzenau commences at 1900 hours. It increases in intensity at 2000 hours and then stops abruptly ten minutes later. I rush outside with my men. This is the typical situation before an attack. We listen in the darkness. Nothing! There is total silence across the front of the entire battalion.

29 October: The night passes without Ivan disturbing us. There is light on the horizon above Matzhausen. It is relatively quiet outside. I decide to risk a visit to the battalion. I take one of my messengers with me. The other remains at the command post. He is to fire a white flare if anything happens. It isn't far to the battalion command post.

Under the cover provided by the houses, we leave Schwarzenau and disappear into a depression to the west. We reach a muddy ditch and continue further to the south-west.

The messenger suddenly says, 'There's a dead man over there!' We go the few steps over to the spot he's indicated. A 'Grossdeutschland' grenadier trooper lies in the grass. It isn't clear where he's been hit. His papers have already been taken away. Also missing is his identification tag. That meant his unit knows about his death.

I find Captain Teusen at the command post and report. The commander is of the view that we'll soon be relieved. If only the Almighty can hear his words!

Fallschirm-Panzerfüsilierbataillon 2 'Hermann Göring' – 8/186/412 (a total of 606)

Staff and strength as of November 1944

Battalion staff	4/2/14
Battalion commander	Major Arnold/Captain Wolf
Adjutant	Second Lieutenant Knoblauch
Orderly officer	Master Sergeant Ehlen
Signal officer	Second Lieutenant Gross
Medical officer	First Lieutenant Naumann

5th Company (supply company)	2/44/59
Company commander	Captain Klingbeil
Fourth general staff officer	First Lieutenant Lingrön

1st Company   /31/89
Company commander   Sergeant Tischler
I Platoon   Sergeant Scheler
II Platoon   Sergeant Heidenreich
III Platoon   Sergeant Quentin
IV Platoon   Sergeant Prikowitsch

2nd Company   /43/80
Company commander   Master Sergeant Rapp
I Platoon   Sergeant Schröder
II Platoon   Sergeant Schuster
III Platoon   Sergeant Trippens
IV Platoon   Sergeant Ortlieb

3rd Company   2/39/92
Company commander   First Lieutenant Kailff
I Platoon   Second Lieutenant Klodt
II Platoon   Sergeant Bader
III Platoon   Sergeant Meyer
IV Platoon   Sergeant Tatenhorst

4th Company   /27/78
Company commander   Master Sergeant Staguhn
Flak Platoon   Sergeant Bekemacker
Mortar Platoon   Sergeant Major Glück
Light Infantry Platoon   Sergeant Wilshues

My messenger looks around in the meantime and comes back with a small bundle of letters for the company. It is quite remarkable that the field post was still in operation.

I am back in the cellar of my command post at 08.15. Mortar fire is being directed against Schwarzenau and the company's positions. Time passes slowly. I won't be able to visit my men in their open positions during daylight hours. They crouch in their foxholes and are hardly able to move. Only after dark, and when the enemy fire abates, can my men get moving. Seeing to their needs isn't easy under such circumstances.

It is dark once more. I inspect the positions and, with the help of my messengers, see to the distribution of what meagre rations are available.

We are subjected to heavy artillery fire shortly after midnight. Our cellar shakes as if there is an earthquake. Preserving jars fall off a shelf in the next room. The cellar soon smells of applesauce.

30 October: Our positions are systematically bombarded by Soviet artillery. Daken and Peterstal are also under heavy fire. It seems to me that an attack is imminent.

The night is over. The attack that we feared would take place at dawn hasn't materialised. The five farmsteads of Schwarzenau have been subjected to the concentrated fire of Soviet artillery since 1000 hours. We'll be finished if our house receives a direct hit. The cellar ceiling is too weak.

One of my men staggers in from outside at midday. He is wounded. A splinter has hit his left shoulder. I examine the wound. Thank God he hasn't lost any blood. He is bandaged in a makeshift manner and then goes to crouch in the corner. He'll only be able to be transported away after sunset. He'll have to wait until then.

The enemy fire dies down. Only every now and then is there a blast on the village road. I set off to see the men in the foxholes.

The engine of an armoured car can be heard from the direction of Preussischnassau (Egglenischken). The battalion Volkswagen stops in front of me shortly afterwards. The driver is in a hurry. He doesn't trust the momentary calm. In great haste, he unloads a canister of coffee (or rather a coffee substitute) and a box of ammunition with bread and sausages. The wounded man climbs aboard, and then the Volkswagen disappears into the night as quickly as it arrived.

The men in the foxholes are happy about the hot drink that looks like coffee but isn't. It is the first time in days that they've had something warm.

1 November: The nights are bitterly cold. I've just arrived back from inspecting the positions and decide to try to get some sleep.

I'm not sure how long I sleep for. Rifle fire wakes me up. I go outside, but it's quiet again. Remarkably quiet.

Feeling tired, I return to the cellar and hope there won't be any more surprises during the night.

Footsteps again on the cellar stairs. I reach for my pistol.

Two of my men stand in the doorway. One of them is hardly able to stand unsupported. I can see even in the dim illumination provided by the Hindenburg light that one side of his head is wounded. He is shivering all over. I stand and sit him down in my chair.

'What happened?'

The second man answers: 'An assault detachment ambushed us. I'd just climbed out of my foxhole to relieve myself when Ivan pounced. They must have been lying in wait in front of our foxhole for a long time. Everything happened without a sound.' He pointed to his comrade. 'They hit him on the head, dragged him out of the foxhole and took him away!'

'And how is it that he's here now?'

'The sentry to our left heard noises and shot into the darkness. He obviously hit something. My comrade was able to escape in the confusion.'

The wounded man sits trembling on my chair. His eyes blink, and his jaw is moving. He wants to say something, but no words come out.

I come to a decision. 'Get ready! We'll sweep the area.'

The four of us make our way along the company's front from foxhole to foxhole. The men have been fully woken up by the exchange of fire.

I take a closer look at the foxhole where the wounded man had been. His helmet lies on the ground. He'd taken it off so that he could hear better. It has almost cost him his life.

We cautiously make our way along the suspected route of retreat of the Russian assault detachment. After about 50 metres, I see a dark object lying on the ground in front of us. It could be a man, judging by its size. With fingers on our triggers, we slowly approach one step at a time.

Only a few more steps. There is no doubt someone is lying there. I glance around and then go right up to him.

It is a Russian. Next to him is a submachine gun. I shake him a little. He is dead.

'Let's pick him up! We'll take him back with us.'

With considerable effort, we carry this gigantic man over the rising terrain into Schwarzenau. We check his pockets under the cover provided by a house wall. We find photos of girls and clippings of articles bearing his name. I can tell that much despite the Cyrillic script. He wears various medals on his chest, including a red star. He was obviously an important member of his regiment.

This Soviet man has traipsed from somewhere near the Volga or perhaps from somewhere else, all the way to East Prussia, just as we had done to Stalingrad, only to have an accidental hit put an end to his career. It occurs to me that he'll never see Berlin. I don't say that out loud, and this thought certainly doesn't give me any satisfaction.

I bundle the dead Russian's papers and medals into a small package and hand it to the messenger who will next be setting off for the battalion. Perhaps the divisional third general staff officer will be interested in it.

It is quiet once more. I try to get some sleep.

2 November: In the early hours of the morning, Ivan opens fire with heavy artillery on the small number of houses in Schwarzenau. I hold the morning messenger back for the time being so that he won't be put in any unnecessary danger.

Even in our cellar are we can clearly hear the howling of the guns. There is an infernal noise from the village road outside. Only at noon does the company messenger manage to make it to the battalion.

Official word comes from the commander in the evening: 'We are to be relieved tomorrow morning!' I'll only believe it if the relief unit actually arrives.

3 November: It is shortly after midnight. I go outside with a messenger to pass on the good news.

I hear howling the moment I step outside. The messenger and I take cover right away. The howling and the explosions are nonstop. They are caused by shells from German rocket launchers that have somehow fallen into Ivan's hands.

There is a cessation of fire after a few minutes. We go outside again. Although it's dark, it is clear that the roof of the house next door has collapsed onto the road. I go from foxhole to foxhole and inform the men that we are to be relieved. There are various reactions. Some are doubtful and say so in no uncertain terms. Others feel revived by the news. The rest are so apathetic that my words are acknowledged without any emotion.

Something is happening on the village road at 0300 hours. I go up the cellar stairs and come across an officer of the 2nd Reconnaissance Battalion 'Hermann Göring'.

I describe to him the situation in brief and the location of the front, or at least as far as it is known to me in the darkness.

The relief company arrive ten minutes later. While not at full combat strength, it is more complete in terms of personnel than my worn-out bunch of men.

The relief is carried out quickly. Ivan doesn't notice a thing, and we make our way silently to the battalion. The other companies have already arrived. We soon come across three medium-sized trucks parked on the side of the road. We are both delighted and surprised to learn that we will be transported on those trucks. The entire battalion will be able to fit into them. I estimate the strength of the battalion to be about 60 men. No wonder we are being pulled out of the front.

We get on board and the journey on the open trucks through the cold night air begins. Schwarzenau and the front line around Daken are under fire from Soviet artillery.

I sleep for some time. When I wake up, we are driving through Gumbinnen. The journey comes to an end after another seven kilometres. We get out of the vehicles. Kubbeln is the name of this small village, where we will be staying for a short time. It lies on the Gumbinnen–Insterburg road.

The companies are distributed among the few houses. One house per company! How the times have changed. I think of the large barracks complexes in the Reich.

I urgently want to wash and shave. I am shocked when I look in the mirror. I hardly recognise myself: bearded, dirty and bleary-eyed.

The men want rations once they've had enough sleep. I go to look for the man who'll be responsible for this. I find a staff sergeant in a sparsely furnished office. I ask him where I'll find the company sergeant major.

'The company sergeant major has left for Königsberg with the men of the old regimental cadre. There was supposed to be some order to that effect. I don't have any further details. I have taken over the duties of the company sergeant major.'

I can't quite believe what he's told me, but I ask him to continue to perform the duties of the company sergeant major until the matter has been resolved.

I look around the village. I can only see a few of the old paratroopers left.

A decision has to be made. I reach for the field telephone and call Division.

After a few attempts, I manage to get a first lieutenant on the line, possibly an orderly officer. I learn from our conversation that the withdrawal of the parachute troops hasn't been carried out on the orders of Division. The first lieutenant requests of me that the remnants of the battalion be kept where they are until the new commander arrives the next day.

I am somewhat shocked but don't say anything.

4 November: I step out the door of my quarters just as a Volkswagen command car drives up.

A major gets out. 'I'm looking for a Second Lieutenant Knoblauch!'

'That's me, Major!'

'I am the new commander. My name is Arnold. Let's go into your company's orderly room and discuss what is needed.'

I lead the way and invite the major, now my new commander, to come in.

We sit down, and Major Arnold begins immediately. 'Second Lieutenant Knoblauch, from now you are my adjutant. Our task is the reorganisation of the battalion. Division has promised that the first replacements of officers and men will arrive this afternoon. We will talk later about the provision of vehicles and weapons. Any questions?'

'No questions, Major, although I should point out that I have never been an adjutant and have no training in this regard.'

'That doesn't matter one bit, my dear fellow. Common sense and a strong will are more important.'

I'm not so sure and simply take note of the major's statement in silence.

The commander stands and asks me to come with him. 'We will now look for accommodation for the headquarters.'

The headquarters are set up by the afternoon sufficiently that work can begin.

I go to the commander. 'Do you have orders, Major? The first 50 replacements of men have arrived.'

'No, I have no orders. You may act independently. That also applies in the future. We are a divisional battalion. Your authority as adjutant is extensive. Make use of it!'

I stand to attention and leave.

'Divisional battalion' and 'extensive authority' indeed. A commander who doesn't have any orders is a novelty for me.

I sit down in my office, take a few sheets of typewriter paper and draft an order of battle for the battalion. Official documents have been promised for the following morning, but I can't wait that long.

I organised all the new arrivals into their units before midnight. Platoon and squad leaders have been assigned off the cuff.

5 November: I drive to Division Headquarters and am given actual documents such as tables of organisation and so on. Feeling a bit wiser, I go to work.

The first replacements of officers have arrived. They are almost exclusively officers who haven't come from the infantry. This causes me some concern.

A ray of hope in these gloomy times is the fact that the non-commissioned officers who have been appointed company sergeant majors are doing their jobs well. Also, the battalion clerk is a judicious man.

After assigning another 100 men in the afternoon, I go to the commander and report on how things are going.

Major Arnold nods in satisfaction and doesn't ask any questions. He signs the reports on combat strength and the requests for equipment without properly looking at them.

Only then do we learn that fighting has been taking place in the vicinity of Goldap since the day before and that the town has only just now been retaken.

The formations involved are 5. Panzerdivision, the 50. Infanteriedivision, and elements of Panzergrenadierdivision 'Grossdeutschland'.

6 November: The battalion is now at a combat strength of 400 men. Apart from seeing to the formation and organisation of the companies, I have come up with a training schedule. The commander has approved everything without comment.

There is a radio report on 8 November about the use of V-2 rockets against southern England.

The commander calls for me in the evening.

'Mr Knoblauch, tomorrow is 9 November [*TN*: the anniversary of the Munich Putsch, commemorated by the Nazi Party]. You know what that means. Orders have come from above that the units stationed in the rear area be made aware of this in the appropriate manner. I'm feeling sick, so you take care of it!'

I am at a loss for words. I am no party speaker!

I give the matter some thought and then summon the company commanders.

'Gentlemen, the commander has ordered me to say a few words about 9 November tomorrow. For this purpose, the battalion will assemble here in front of the headquarters tomorrow morning at 1000 hours. We will march out into the meadow on the southern outskirts of the village. I will say what needs to be said to the companies, which will be lined up in an open square. Do you have any questions?'

There are no questions. My audience is astonished.

9 November: The battalion assembles. The battalion commander is still sick. I receive the report from the commander of the 3rd Company and see to it that the troops move off towards the meadow on the outskirts of the village of Kubbeln.

The battalion stands before me at 10.30. I take a few steps forward so that I won't have to speak too loudly.

The men look at me more or less without expression. Some of the officers, however, seem to be keen to hear what I have to say on this National Socialist day of remembrance in such difficult times. I have no doubt that I'll be regarded as politically aligned once I am done.

'Comrades, let us consider the difficult situation faced by our Fatherland on this day. Let us remember that here, in East Prussia, the Red Army set foot on the soil of the German Reich for the first time. Let us not forget what it means for the population to fall into the hands of the Russians. The events of Nemmersdorf and Schulzenwalde are only three weeks behind us. Everyone knows what happened. It is not only the soldierly but also the moral duty of each and every one of us to bring the Soviet onslaught to a halt here on the border of the Reich with the utmost commitment. Fusiliers, let me tell you one thing from experience, and that is that this task can only be carried out if we stick together, if each man can rely on the man next to him! We must all ensure that the fusilier battalion becomes a real fighting community in the shortest possible time. We stand in the tradition of the tried and tested I Battalion of the Fallschirmjägerregiment 16, a formation that was still engaged in combat against the enemy only a few days ago. We want to prove ourselves worthy of this tradition. May every man feel that the battalion is his home and that his company is his family. Let us get to work! Let us do our duty!'

I feel relieved now that that is done. I have the troops move off. They sing as they march back to Kubbeln. The easterly wind carries the rumble of artillery fire over to us from the nearby front.

I go to see the commander and report that his order for 9 November has been carried out. He nods. That is it. No questions!

11 November: Further replacements have arrived. The strength of the battalion has grown to more than 500 men. Systematic infantry training has become problematic. There is a lack of qualified instructors. Shooting and squad combat training are given priority. Exercises in platoon or company formation are still a long way off.

I am under the impression that the commander has no understanding of the problems we face. I can't ignore the fact that he feels no connection with the infantry. He will certainly have his merits, but he is completely out of place here.

14 November: The commander is still unwell. He even refuses to answer the telephone. I am having some difficulty shielding him from repeated inquiries from Division.

Artillery fire from the Goldap area becomes stronger in the evening.

Dr Naumann sends me to see a specialist in Insterburg on 15 November. I've been experiencing considerable pain in my left eye socket for several days. It is possible that there are small splinters that have been in my head since I was wounded in September 1943, which are now pressing on a nerve.

I come back the next day with no result. The examination in the hospital hasn't revealed anything. I've probably been physically and mentally overwhelmed over the course of the previous few weeks.

The battalion is to be brought to the front, step by step. Rear defensive positions will be taken up as early as the next day on the Schulzenwalde–Eggenhof road.

There won't be any contact with the enemy there. I am happy about that. It means that we'll still have some time to press ahead with training.

17 November: The battalion departs Kubbeln on foot in the early hours of the morning and establishes positions to the east of Bismarckhöh in the afternoon.

I drive ahead in a Volkswagen command car and set up the command post to the east of the Bismarck tower. Signal communications with Division are established.

It is still light, so I inspect the shelters that have been dug in the ground by the companies.

The commander has retreated into his hideaway behind my office.

18 November: It is 1000 hours. The battalion clerk rushes into my room. 'Second Lieutenant, the brigadier is outside!'

Soon Brigadier Schmalz is standing in the doorway, the commander of Fallschirm-Panzerkorps 'Hermann Göring'. I notice the Oak Leaves at his neck.

I don't get a chance to report. The corps commander approaches me quickly, 'Are you the adjutant?'

'Yes, Brigadier!'

'Where is your commander?'

'The commander is in bed. He is sick.'

'Go to him and tell him that I want to speak to him immediately. Immediately!'

I go through the door into the adjoining room. 'Major, the corps commander is here and wants to speak to you immediately.'

The major has barely moved when the corps commander comes in. He turns to me and says: 'Second Lieutenant, please leave us!' The door slams shut. I step back a little.

I hear a few scraps of the conversation on the other side of the door. The corps commander's voice becomes louder and then stops suddenly.

The door opens. Brigadier Schmalz comes out and walks past me without saying a word. He disappears as quickly as he arrived.

The battalion commander calls to me: 'Mr Knoblauch, I'm not in the best of health. The brigadier is of the opinion that I should go to hospital immediately. Have my personal belongings packed and the driver ordered for 1100 hours.'

The driver is on time. Major Arnold bids me farewell, gets into the command car and drives off.

I receive a telephone call from the divisional orderly officer a little later. 'Second Lieutenant Knoblauch, I'm phoning to inform you that Captain Wolf of the 4th Regiment will take command of the fusilier battalion from today.'

A vehicle from the 4th Regiment drives up to the command post at 1300 hours. I go outside.

A captain gets out of the car and approaches me at a brisk pace. 'You must be the adjutant. I am Captain Wolf and from now on the commander of this battalion. I assume that you have been informed of this by Division. Let's go inside.'

Captain Wolf is certainly not the kind of superior who has 'no orders'. I estimate him to be about 34 years old, and he looks like a large and dynamic fellow. He comes straight to the point. 'Mr Knoblauch, immediately gather documents regarding numbers of personnel, assignments of officers and inventories of vehicles and weaponry. I assume the battalion has horses as well?'

'Yes, the battalion has horses. The soldiers are already talking about the "Parachute Pony Corps"!'

Captain Wolf settles in. I notice that he has unusually little baggage.

20 November: I see to the distribution of the orders for the day. Although Captain Wolf may have been assigned only the role of battalion commander, for us he is simply 'the commander' due to the forcefulness of his personality.

I present him an order from Division, according to which the battalion is to appoint one of its officers as a National Socialist Leadership Officer.

Captain Wolf reads the order carefully and then turns to me. 'I have looked at the assignments of officers. I was also with the companies yesterday to get to know these gentlemen. Master Sergeant Ehlen will be transferred immediately to the headquarters as orderly officer. Inform Division that he will also be appointed as National Socialist Leadership Officer. I myself will decide the sphere of control of this appointment. I will tell Ehlen personally where his duties begin and where they end.'

And that's it. A clear decision has been made!

It should be noted that Ehlen has never done anything that resembles what might be required of a National Socialist Leadership Officer. I also doubt that he'll be interested in it.

It has become unpleasantly cold since yesterday. Winter has arrived!

21 November: Heavy rain falls on our positions. The terrain on either side of the paved roads becomes impassable.

The corps commander visits us in the afternoon. He obviously wants to gain an impression of the battalion's situation after the change of leadership.

22 November: Among the mail that has arrived is a notification of my promotion to first lieutenant. I sort out the mail and present it to the battalion commander. Captain Wolf comes into my room a few minutes later. 'Second Lieutenant Knoblauch, you will have noticed when looking through the mail that you have been promoted. For the sake of good order, I hereby formally announce your promotion to first lieutenant. Congratulations!'

'Thank you, Captain!'

In the afternoon we receive a visit from Colonel Söth, an army officer who is a member of staff of 2. Division 'Hermann Göring'.

We receive further visitors. Lieutenant Colonel Kluge, the commander of the 4th Regiment, is our guest on 23 November. I'd been informed by Captain Wolf that the regimental commander had been awarded the Knight's Cross in 1943. He made a name for himself as the commander of 'Detachements Kluge' during the campaign in Norway in April 1940. It doesn't take long for me to figure out that the captain and lieutenant colonel are old acquaintances.

Quite unexpectedly, Captain Wolf places a bottle of red wine on the table. 'Lieutenant Colonel, my adjutant was promoted to first lieutenant yesterday. With your permission, I would like to pour us some wine on this occasion!'

'Please do!' The lieutenant colonel stands up, shakes my hand and congratulates me.

We don't stop at the first bottle of Beaujolais. We've certainly had enough by the time the third one is nearly empty.

Lieutenant Colonel Kluge turns to me in good cheer. 'Mr Knoblauch, you have no idea of the qualities of your commander. I regard him to be a genius of elocution. You should see him when he quotes from *Faust* by heart. Mr Wolf, please demonstrate for us!'

The commander is reluctant at first, but he soon comes round:

Again you show yourselves, you wavering Forms, …

He goes from 'Prelude' to 'Prologue in Heaven' and then to Scene I.

Ah! Now I've done Philosophy,
I've finished Law and Medicine,
And sadly even Theology:
Taken fierce pains, from end to end.
Now here I am, a fool for sure!
No wiser than I was before: …
[*TN*: The translation of Faust is by A. S. Kline (2003).]

He continues for some time. We've stopped drinking. Once Captain Wolf has finished, Lieutenant Colonel Kluge reaches for his glass. 'Mr Wolf, we thank you. That was magnificent as always!'

I'm impressed. I've never heard a recitation of such quality.

Those of the battalion adjutants and company commanders who are available are ordered to take part in a divisional map exercise.

The so-called 'large-scale battle exercise' is played out on the sand table. It involves a measure to keep losses to a minimum by withdrawing the troops from the main line of resistance when the enemy starts a sudden concentration of artillery fire.

The troops, apart from a few elements, will fall back to a second line (the Nelke Line) shortly before the anticipated enemy attack and will then launch a counter-attack soon after the cessation of the enemy artillery fire in order to retake the positions along the main line of resistance.

The idea is convincing. However, I can see difficulties regarding the state of the newly formed units. Knowledge of routine and experience at the front, both of which are of great importance in such a situation, will be lacking in many cases.

25 November: A battalion messenger enters the command post at noon. 'First Lieutenant, there's a civilian outside with his son. He'd like to speak with an officer.'

I go outside. In front of me stands a man with his boy, who looks to be about 12 years old.

'What can I do for you?'

The man speaks with an East Prussian accent. 'First Lieutenant, would your soldiers be able to help us dig up my wife so that we can bury her properly? She was killed by the Russians and buried in the ground by the road behind us. I want to take her in my cart to Schulzenwalde so that she can be given a decent burial.'

I swallow uncomfortably. The boy is pale and emotionless.

I give the man two of my soldiers. He thanks me, tips his worn cap, and leaves.

There is a visitor for me! My messenger from the former 2nd Company of the Fallschirmjägerregiment 16, Corporal Münekhoff, suddenly appears in the doorway. 'I happened to be passing by, First Lieutenant, and thought I should say hello!' I am delighted to see him. Münekhoff certainly wouldn't have visited had I left a bad impression on the 2nd Company.

1 December: Winter has properly set in. It is snowing.

My father died three years ago yesterday. I think he was spared a great deal.

The commander has gone to the divisional headquarters. To be discussed is the allocation of heavy weaponry. The armament at our disposal is still insufficient.

My left eye socket is in pain again. Dr Naumann thinks it's necessary that I'm examined by a specialist.

I report this to the commander in the evening. He agrees that I should be admitted to hospital.

2–7 December: Examinations in Tapiau and Königsberg reveal nothing new. Full of disappointment, I return to the battalion.

8 December: A briefing with the company commanders is organised for 1000 hours. The battalion commander lays out his personal recommendation for a 'large-scale order of battle'.

The day is filled with writing letters to the relatives of those who have fallen in the recent fighting. I have to force myself to do this over and over again.

10 December: It is Sunday. Captain Wolf tells me that he wants to be alone for half an hour so that he can drink a cup of tea. He actually has a clean napkin and a Chinese teacup ready for this ritual. Once fully revived, he returns to his military duties with great dynamism.

The amount of paperwork required of an adjutant is certainly extensive. I'd thought myself unsuitable for such work, but this turns out not to be the case.

On 13 December, I am awarded the Ground Assault Badge of the Luftwaffe for my participation in the fighting between Gumbinnen and Goldap. This corresponds roughly to the Infantry Assault Badge.

16 December: Our positions are struck by ground-attack bombers in the early hours of yesterday morning. We don't suffer any casualties.

One thing is certain, though, and that is that the Soviets are aware of the location of our second line (the Nelke Line).

An order arrives from Division according to which we are to assume responsibility for the positions along the front line to the east of Girnen.

The companies are ready to march. Tomorrow, early in the morning, the change of position will be carried out.

17 December: The companies set off at 0300 hours and, spread out in a long line, they march to Girnen via Brauersdorf and Alt Wusterwitz. The battalion commander goes on ahead with his staff.

The command post bunker lies on a reverse slope approximately 500 metres to the north-east of Girnen. The battalion and company commanders converse, and I listen.

It is a relatively quiet night. Only now and then is a shot fired. Flares appear in the sky above Brückental.

The spearhead company arrives at 05.10. The troops that are already at the front are relieved platoon by platoon. We hope that Ivan won't notice anything and won't stir.

The positions lie, depending on the nature of the terrain, 400 to 900 metres in front of the battalion command post with a view of Reichsstrasse 132, which runs from the south-east to the north-west through the village of Brückental.

Understandably, the troops who have been relieved want to leave the area as quickly as possible.

We are alone. The commander has gone forward with two men to visit the companies. I remain to set up the command post properly.

Telegraph communications with Division have been established. There is no radio contact. I wonder what we'll do if a sudden concentration of enemy artillery fire breaks the wire connection.

18 December: The signal troops check the wire connection before dawn.

A messenger arrives from the 2nd Company at 11.10. Two men belonging to the company have been shot dead by snipers.

The commander listens to the messenger's report and then turns to me. 'Draft a battalion order at once that points out this sniper problem. We cannot afford casualties due to carelessness or inexperience.'

The two dead men are brought to the battalion from the company's sector after dark. The company sergeant major of the supply company will take them with him once he's delivered rations, mail and ammunition.

I am astonished by what I hear on the radio. The High Command of the Wehrmacht made the following announcement: 'Strong German forces launched an attack on a wide front from the Siegfried Line at 05.30 on 16 December after brief yet tremendous preparatory fire and overran the forwardmost American positions between the High Fens and the northern part of Luxembourg in the first assault. Offensive combat continues under the protection of strong fighter formations.'

I thought that something like this was no longer possible. Are we stronger than it had previously seemed?

19 December: A man of the 3rd Company is killed this morning by a shot to the head. Captain Wolf is furious and summons the company commander.

20 December: I am on my way back from the 4th Regiment 'Hermann Göring' when Ivan starts to shell the area around our command post with his heavy artillery. The driver manages to get the Volkswagen command car under cover just in time. I wait until there is a brief pause and then dash into the command post bunker.

As I brush the dirt off my combat uniform, I overhear the commander speaking to the signal officer. 'Heeresgruppe Mitte (Army Group Centre) would have collapsed even if the events of 20 July hadn't happened!'

I am somewhat surprised. The staff of the battalion headquarters haven't yet discussed 20 July, its background, or its consequences. None of us knows each other well enough.

The signal officer leaves the shelter. Captain Wolf looks at me. I sense that he expects me to comment on what I've heard.

'Captain, I don't think we have a full enough picture to be able to make a definitive statement. That's my only reservation. Although, truth be told, I am bothered by the fact that soldiers from old Prussian families broke their oath of allegiance. The forefathers of Treskow, Stülpnagel and so on served Frederick the Great. I can't think of a time back then that members of these families broke their oath of allegiance. They would have died for their king if necessary!'

'Mr Knoblauch, no matter how we evaluate the motives behind the assassination attempt, one thing is indisputable, and that is that the Prussian king and the Führer are not comparable figures. The Prussian officers saw themselves as personal representatives of their monarch. They felt themselves to be advocates of their king, regardless of the time or place. The cause of their king was theirs and vice versa. This was the case for the youngest lieutenant and the oldest field marshal. The Führer, however, is not held aloft by the officer corps. Apart from a few exceptions, the officer corps primarily feels itself bound by duty to the Reich. I would go so far as to venture to say that the enormous sacrifices that have been made thus far were not for the Führer but rather for the survival of the Reich. That will continue to be the case for the next few months. Our duty, Mr Knoblauch, lies only to the Reich! And one more thing should not be overlooked, and that is that the officer was the head of state in the Kingdom of Prussia. Today, it is the party man. This has an effect on the nature of the relationship with the head of state and also on the nature of the oath itself. Let us make no mistake that the Russians will confront us in a final battle here in East Prussia in a few weeks. We will go into this battle despite knowing that most of us will not survive. Our actions will certainly not be determined by the oath that binds us to Hitler. We will stand and probably fall here in East Prussia because we want to defend the Reich and its people in a final act of soldierly duty against the Russians. This has nothing to do with the oath of allegiance. It is instead a matter of self-respect. One last thing is that I cannot believe the flawed manner in which Stauffenberg carried out the assassination attempt. It is worse that he sacrificed the lives of his fellow officers and kept himself at a distance. It would be a bit like Second Lieutenant Schneider willingly accepting your death in order to eliminate me. Could you imagine such a thing?'

'No, Captain, certainly not with Second Lieutenant Schneider! But there have been events since 20 July that couldn't have been imagined previously. It seems to me that the officer corps has suffered a severe blow and perhaps even a fatal one, at least as far as its Prussian character is concerned. Only time will tell.'

'Maybe you're right. Let us bring this topic of discussion to a close and conduct ourselves in future as if it had never taken place.'

'It never took place, Captain.'

I turn my attention to my paperwork. The daily reports from the companies have come in. The conversation with the commander has given me food for thought. I can't stop thinking about what he said.

21 December: A reconnaissance patrol of the 3rd Company is sent out in front of our positions in the evening. It is astonishing that the personnel allocated to such a patrol isn't something that had to be specified in orders. There are still volunteers for such operations. This certainly isn't because the entire Fallschirm-Panzerkorps consists of volunteers who are citizens of the German Reich.

24 December: Christmas Eve! I go to see the men along the main line of resistance after nightfall. Flares rise into the sky above Brückental and Husarenberg. A dull light stretches across the vast expanse of snow.

The soldiers are in good cheer.

I arrive back at the command post shortly before midnight.

25 December: First Lieutenant Kalff, commander of the 3rd Company, invites me for a cup of coffee. I have no idea where he got the expensive coffee beans from. I decide it's best not to ask him about it.

26 December: I am in the trench of the 2nd Company at 0300 hours. An assault detachment under the command of a sergeant is ready to blow up a house that stands 200 metres in front of our own positions and that has occasionally been occupied by Ivan at night. The neighbours have been informed. It is soon 03.15. The men of the assault detachment jump over the edge of the trench.

It is 03.45. We listen in the night. I hope that the house is free of enemy forces. A clash with the Russians will usually mean casualties for us.

An explosion shatters the peaceful night at 03.55. Flares are fired from the Russian positions. Machine guns fire into the dimly lit area beyond the front.

It becomes lively in front of our positions ten minutes later. The assault detachment returns. The sergeant reports: 'House blown up! One man wounded!' The wounded man is only slightly injured, thank God.

27 December: Heavy snowfall has started. The men are in the miserable foxholes they've dug along the sides of the trench, and they suffer dreadfully from the bad weather. I see to it that their hot drinks reach them daily before they've gone cold.

29 December: Division constantly maintains contact with its 'home battalion'. We receive a visit from Captain Truckenmüller, presumably at the behest of the divisional first general staff officer.

30 December: Soviet activity in front of our positions suggest that an attack is imminent. The only question is whether it will be merely a local attack or the feared offensive whose objective will be to force a breakthrough into the territory of the Reich.

Division has ordered the construction of reinforced positions. The cold, however, prevents any work on entrenchments. Attempts at blasting to deepen the trenches is unproductive.

31 December: It is 0000 hours, and with that it is also Captain Wolf's birthday. From the depths of his baggage, he pulls out a bottle of Armagnac. Everyone who is present takes a pull on the bottle. In the dim light, I can make out the orderly officer, a signal communication man, the battalion messengers and the signal communication officer.

1945

1 January: I complete a report at 0100 hours on the status of the construction of positions. This report will be sent to Division in the morning.

Before going to get some sleep, I go outside one more time. It is snowing.

The battalion is subjected to heavy mortar fire and fatal sniper activity all day long. After dark, the Russian units in front of us are relieved by new ones.

2 January: My bunker is on fire. The overheated potbellied stove has set fire to the ceiling. It is only with great effort that the fire is brought under control and eventually extinguished.

Snowfall starts in the afternoon that is so thick that visibility is no more than 30 metres.

I hear machine-gun fire at 23.10. It is coming from the sector of the 2nd Company. I go outside and listen in the night. It falls quiet again.

There is a call from the 2nd Company at 23.15: 'Reconnaissance or assault troops repelled in front of our position. No casualties!'

This reconnaissance activity by the Russians indicates once more that an attack is imminent.

The leadership of the battalion is faced with the question of how its young soldiers will conduct themselves under the stress of large-scale combat. It will be the first serious engagement for most of them.

3 January: Russian artillery pounds our positions. The enemy has obviously identified the location of the battalion command post. Heavy chunks of rock fall in the vicinity of our bunkers. Sand filters its way between the beams of the ceiling.

The commander is on the move nonstop during the night. He has seen to the reinforcement of the night trench patrol.

In order to prevent being taken by surprise, we arrange to have our own reconnaissance troops posted before the front every night. This is not so much to conduct reconnaissance of the Soviet positions but rather to ensure the security of the area beyond our front.

4 January: A messenger stumbles into my shelter at 04.15. 'Report from the 3rd Company! Ivan overcame our trench patrol an hour ago. A junior officer and a corporal were probably taken prisoner. No shot was fired. We only found out about this when the next patrol went to take over.'

'And what action has been taken in the meantime?'

'The company commander took a squad into the area beyond the front. The tracks were clear. Our two men were dragged through the snow. There were also traces of blood on the edge of the trench. The junior officer's submachine gun was found 50 metres in front of our positions!'

I go over to the battalion commander, who's only just lain down to get some sleep. Unfortunately, I have to wake him up. 'Captain, Ivan was in the 3rd Company's trench and has carried out a raid against the trench patrol!'

Captain Wolf reaches for his submachine gun, grabs his cap and turns to me as he goes outside: 'I want to see this for myself.' He disappears into the darkness with the messenger from the 3rd Company.

The commander returns at 0600 hours. He hasn't found out anything new.

Dr Naumann invites me for a glass of wine in the evening. Things like this still happen despite Ivan.

The stress of the previous few weeks has taken its toll on me. The lack of sleep almost makes me feel that I am done for.

6 January: It is 0300 hours. Captain Wolf has gone forward to the trenches. An assault detachment from the 2nd Company is going to carry out a raid against a Russian post during the night. This post occupies a protruding 'nose' in the enemy defensive system. I remain at the command post and sit near the field telephone.

I become restless by 03.50. I go outside and listen in the darkness. The assault detachment must have engaged the enemy by now. But it is quiet. Only here and there is there a shot. Everything is strangely calm. I hope our men haven't walked into a trap.

The commander returns at 04.40. I look at him questioningly. He puts his submachine gun down in the corner and says: 'Imagine, Trippens jumped into the trench with his men, only to find that Ivan wasn't there!'

'And what did Sergeant Trippens do then?'

'Well, the only thing he could do in this messed-up situation, and that was to come back silently.'

The commander withdraws. He wants to go to sleep. I am on the telephone for the rest of the night.

8 January: In the morning we receive a visit, quite unexpectedly, from the corps commander. He listens to Captain Wolf's report on the battalion's situation and then suddenly asks me one of his notorious exam questions: 'A 2cm anti-aircraft gun moved into position in the vicinity of Girnen a few days ago. Show me where it is on the map.'

I know only approximately where the anti-aircraft gun stands and can't provide a precise answer. The general notices immediately, of course, that I wasn't fully aware of the situation and turns to the battalion commander. 'Captain Wolf, surely you know where the anti-aircraft gun is?'

Captain Wolf does indeed know. He is more frequently out and about than I am. The general grins and turns again to the battalion commander. 'Wolf, I expected that you'd know, but your adjutant has no idea!'

The corps commander reaches for his white fur cap, salutes and leaves. Captain Wolf and I look at one another, somewhat taken aback.

10 January: I was busy with the supply company yesterday. I take the opportunity to have a look at the anti-aircraft gun emplacement that brought the general so much joy.

The 3rd Company report two men killed by snipers.

A meeting is held with the company commanders at 1400 hours. The battalion commander gets straight to the point: 'It is clear from the frequent casualties inflicted on us by snipers, with two more dead this morning, that the men are still moving around too carelessly in their positions. Make it clear to them that recklessness is not the same thing as courage! I would like to know from the commander of the supply company how the latest divisional order, which deals with the burial of the dead in the military cemetery in Gumbinnen, has been carried out so far.'

Captain Klingbeil reports: 'The divisional order says that the footwear, uniforms and camouflage jackets that belonged to the fallen are to be recovered. Burial shrouds will be provided by the division.'

The commander interrupts: 'What do you mean by "will be provided"? If I understand you correctly, Mr Klingbeil, these shrouds haven't arrived yet. How have the fallen from the last few days been buried?'

Captain Klingbeil looks uncomfortable. 'Captain, it's true the shrouds haven't arrived yet. I was therefore only able to carry out the first part of the divisional order. I have had the clothing removed from the fallen.'

The commander finds this unsettling. 'You haven't had them buried naked, have you?'

'No, Captain,' says Klingbeil with a look of distress on his face. 'I had the dead wrapped in straw, or in straw mats, so to speak. The burial unit in Gumbinnen didn't object to this.'

A wave of discontent sweeps through the shelter. The commander of the 3rd Company, First Lieutenant Kalff, can't contain himself. 'This is a disgrace!'

Captain Wolf, who is just as upset as everyone else, speaks again. 'Mr Kalff, I agree with you on this matter. Nevertheless, I expect that you will be careful in your choice of words in future.' He continues: 'Although I personally do not care if one day I am taken to Gumbinnen as a bundle of straw, it is my order that our fallen will be buried in their uniforms. This is what will be done until the burial shrouds arrive from the division.'

The case is closed. The shrouds never arrive.

12 January: All the companies report that there is movement in the Russian positions. At 14.30, Ivan fires smoke shells. We anticipate that he will launch a major attack. The battalion is on the alert.

The Soviet Winter Offensive and the End of the 2. Fallschirm-Panzerfüsilierbataillon 'Hermann Göring', January 1945

2. Fallschirm-Panzerfüsilierbataillon (2nd Parachute Panzer Fusilier Battalion) 'Hermann Göring'

Battalion commander	Captain Wolf (wounded 25 January 1945)
Adjutant	First Lieutenant Knoblauch (wounded 25 January 1945)
Signal officer	Second Lieutenant Schneider (missing in action 25 January 1945)
Orderly officer	Second Lieutenant Küchel (missing in action January/February 1945)
Battalion doctor	First Lieutenant Naumann (whereabouts unknown)
1st Company	Captain Preuss (killed in action 19 January 1945)
2nd Company	Second Lieutenant Rapp (missing in action January/February 1945)
3rd Company	First Lieutenant Kalff (whereabouts unknown)
4th Company	Master Sergeant Staguhn (whereabouts unknown)
5th Supply Company	Captain Klingbeil (missing in action February 1945)

13 January: A deafening blast wakes me from my half sleep. I look at my watch. It is 07.01.

I go carefully for a look outside the shelter. It is snowing a little. I can feel the cold immediately.

The artillery fire to our left has intensified. It is slowly sweeping towards our positions. I jump back into the shelter to telephone the companies. The connection is broken.

Captain Wolf has gone outside with his binoculars and is observing the terrain in front of our positions to the west of Brückental.

It will be impossible to command the battalion while the artillery fire continues with such intensity. We don't have any radio equipment.

The fighting subsides in the early afternoon. The maintenance men have gone to repair the wire connections. The number of outages are still fairly limited.

14 January: It is dawn. Russian ground-attack aircraft approach at low altitude and strike our positions.

The left wing of the battalion is subjected to the fire of heavy batteries.

Time passes slowly. It is unfortunate that our heavy company is still not yet fully equipped. Only the mortar platoon is fully operational.

Across the front of the 1st Company, approximately 600 metres to the south of Husarenberg, our assault guns put four T-34s out of action. Black smoke engulfs the battlefield. To our south-east, near Peterstal, German counter-thrusts are underway.

It is already apparent that this Soviet offensive is being carried out as a war of attrition, with all the usual wear and tear. But we don't have anything else that can be worn out. Our actions are largely determined by improvisation. On 11 January, shortly before the commencement of this offensive, we'd used a truck to tow agricultural equipment like harrows and seed drills back and forth along the road to the north of Girnen to simulate the sound of tank tracks. Utterly pathetic!

15 January: We are now bearing the brunt of the offensive. The battalion command post lies well within the range of fire of the Soviet guns. Sand falls between the beams of the shelter ceiling.

A messenger from the 3rd Company enters the shelter. He is dragging a Russian behind him by the sleeve.

The news isn't good. Ivan has occupied the company's trench. First Lieutenant Kalff is trying to organise a counter-assault. The number of casualties has increased in the meantime.

The prisoner looks around anxiously. I push him onto an ammunition box. The man trembles with fear. He is obviously afraid of being shot, which is no doubt what would have happened if our roles had been reversed.

A wounded man is brought in. His thigh is bleeding heavily. The Russian becomes more unsettled. He blinks anxiously. He reaches into his breast pocket and pulls out a small folder with pictures. One of the worn photos shows him surrounded by his large family. He gestures in an attempt to make it clear that we should keep him alive for his family.

The commander speaks to him. 'You don't seem to have understood that the Germanskis don't shoot prisoners. Just make sure your commissar doesn't get a hold of you later!'

The Russian hasn't understood a single word, but he seems to have calmed down. Maybe he did understand. He is taken to the rear area after dark.

Captain Wolf approaches me. 'Given that we have no reserves available, the battalion itself will attack tomorrow morning from its current position with the objective of reoccupying the main line of resistance in the front trench. We have no support from heavy weaponry. I will go with the 2nd Company. The attack will begin at 04.30. See to it that the companies are informed! Should I be taken out, you will assume command of the battalion until a decision is made by the division.'

I sit down in a corner of the shelter and draft a battalion order for the attack.

The messengers set off for the companies shortly after 2000 hours. They've been given the express order to report back to me after completing their tasks. I want to make sure that the company commanders actually receive the battalion order.

There is flickering light above the front. Flares drift lazily in the sky. Tracer ammunition from machine guns sweep the landscape from one side to the other and back again.

16 January: The battalion commander goes to visit the companies at 0200 hours. It can hardly be called a front line any more.

I stand above my shelter at 04.30 and peer over the edge of the slope that provides the command post with some cover.

Frantic shooting starts abruptly 500 metres in front of me. The battalion has commenced the attack.

Then I hear the explosions of hand grenades. That means close combat.

It is still dark and it's not yet clear what is happening in the positions ahead. I go back into the shelter and pick up the telephone. The connections with the 1st and 3rd Companies are broken. With great luck, I am able to get the 2nd Company on the line. A corporal answers. He can't say much about the situation. The battle is still underway. The firefight can be heard clearly over the telephone. I ask the corporal if there are any casualties.

'This part of the trench is full of dead and wounded. Ivan has pushed forward against our own attack!'

There is nothing to be done in this situation. The medics are already doing what they can.

Ivan has reacted. His artillery is targeting the area between the front line and the command post. The noise of battle is overwhelming. My shelter shakes. The flame of the candle in front of me flickers.

The firing subsides at 05.20 and then stops completely. I go outside. Captain Wolf comes towards me. 'Knoblauch, that didn't work. Ivan cannot be dealt with without heavy weaponry. The companies have suffered heavy casualties and are having great difficulty in holding the line we've withdrawn to. Send a messenger with a report on the new situation to the 4th Company in Girnen immediately so that the 8cm mortars can intervene when the Russians press their attack. Staguhn can decide for himself when to open fire. The wire connection has been broken.'

The recommencement of artillery fire drives us into the shelter. We have lost contact with the 4th Regiment, the formation to our left, and the last reconnaissance patrol has returned without having been able to do anything about it.

A corporal appears on the stairs leading into the shelter at 08.10. 'Tanks have broken through on the left wing!'

Captain Wolf and I rush outside. Indeed, 500 metres to our left, there are three T-34s. Their barrels point in the direction of Mount Husaren (Hill 121.8). We can't do anything. We can't even inform the neighbouring formation, as we have no idea where it is. It seems to me that our left flank is exposed. If Ivan pivots in our direction, we're done for. But he doesn't pivot.

The lull in the fighting gives us the opportunity to recover the wounded. The entire supply company is committed to the task of transporting them to the dressing station behind Girnen. Dr Naumann and his medics have their hands full.

The reports from the companies arrive at noon. Their combat strength has diminished alarmingly. Casualties amount to more than 50 per cent.

It is dark again. The noise of battle has subsided.

The night is over. Ivan hasn't attacked. He has suffered remarkably heavy casualties.

It has become unusually quiet on the right wing of the battalion. The commander turns to me and says: 'Knoblauch, find out where the right flank company is. No shots have been fired there for an hour.'

I set off with three messengers and two signal communication men. We head south in a line, taking cover behind the hill that also shields the battalion command post. It is snowing. Visibility extends no more than 20 metres. I've done a good job in memorising the map. It would have been pointless to take it with me in this snowstorm.

We come across a barn after 250 metres. We approach slowly and listen. The snow absorbs every sound. An eerie silence surrounds us.

I peer carefully around the southern corner of the barn. We can vaguely hear someone speaking. We can make out the outlines of shadows. The snow is falling so heavily that we can't tell whether they are Russian or German.

Several figures make their way to the north along a field road less than 20 metres in front of us. It is impossible to make them out clearly.

I have my finger on the trigger of my submachine gun. One of my men comes closer to me. 'Should we shoot?' he asks. I shake my head. The thought of possibly shooting my own comrades is unbearable.

The shadows disappear in the snow. I haven't made a decision and am feeling dissatisfied.

We carefully move forward through the snow. We cross a field track and reach a farmstead a few hundred metres further on. It lies approximately halfway between Girnen and Brückental.

We are in luck and come across the remnants of the right flank company. The company commander says: 'Ivan is in a gully 150 metres ahead of us. He tried to dislodge us twice during the night. Provided we have ammunition, we'll be able to fight him off. The combat strength of the company is 49 men.'

That number had been 120 men four days previously. I bid the company commander farewell and promise to do anything in my power to see to the delivery of rations and ammunition.

When I get as far as the Girnen–Brückental road, I decide to give up my attempt to establish contact with the neighbouring formation on the right.

18 January: Sudden artillery fire at 06.15 forces us into action. Ivan wants to destroy our positions using all of the materiel at his disposal. The terrain between the companies and the command post, which is only 200 metres wide, is subjected to nonstop heavy fire.

The artillery fire subsides shortly after 0700 hours. A few MG 42 machine guns hammer away in front of us. Russian infantry forces are advancing.

The commander goes outside and observes what is happening on the battlefield through his binoculars.

We don't have any reserves. It seems to me that Captain Wolf wants to bolster the resolve of the fusilier troops through his presence. He can't do more than that!

Wounded men have been arriving from the front in the meantime. Some of them lie in my shelter. I am greatly concerned that we might be overrun by Ivan before we have the chance to take our wounded comrades to safety.

By 1300 hours, the companies have repelled three assaults of battalion strength. We've suffered heavy casualties. Those who've fallen can't be recovered. This is an unmistakable indication that our front is on the verge of collapse.

19 January: Heavy artillery fire commences again at sunrise. The battalion commander sits on a crate and looks thoughtfully at the map in front of him.

The impacts of shells from Soviet automatic guns can be heard outside. Then the tarpaulin at the entrance to the shelter is pulled aside and the commander of the 1st Company stumbles in.

The unshaven and overtired battalion commander is suddenly wide awake. 'Where's your company, Captain Preuss?'

'Most of the men have fallen. The rest are retreating. We cannot hold out any longer!'

The battalion commander breathes heavily. 'Preuss, you will continue to hold out.'

Captain Preuss silently goes back outside. The battalion commander looks at me but says nothing.

A tried and tested company commander lost his nerve for a moment just now. Who could claim that such a thing will never happen to them? This incident bothers me more than I want to admit.

The battalion commander goes out a little later to visit the units on the right wing of the battalion.

The fire from the enemy's automatic guns increases in intensity.

A messenger from the 1st Company rushes breathlessly into the shelter at 09.30. 'Ivan got into our trench with about 100 men! Captain Preuss was killed during the counter-attack!'

I get the completely exhausted man to sit down on an ammunition box and ask: 'Can you tell me where the 1st Company is at the moment?'

'I can't say for sure. There's no one left in the old position. I think we're already on the same hill as that of the battalion command post.'

I grab my submachine gun to go and have a look at the situation outside, but then Captain Wolf comes in. I report to him the death of Captain Preuss and inform him of the situation of the 1st Company.

The commander makes an effort to keep his emotions over the death of Captain Preuss under control and then says to me: 'You will stay here at the command post and hold the reins. I will go out to the 1st Company with the messenger to see what's really going on there.'

Soviet artillery fire continues unabated.

The commander returns two hours later. 'Knoblauch, the 1st Company has ceased to exist. The sections of trench that I could see are full of dead men, both German and Russian. No more shots are being fired there. The casualties suffered by the Russian infantry are obviously so heavy that they don't have the strength to press the attack, at least for the time being. I have pulled back the left wing of the battalion and have positioned its front so that it is facing to the north. Mark that on the map!'

I can't shake the uncomfortable feeling that the formations to our left and right are no longer in their positions.

The commander sends for me at 1500 hours. 'You will go with the four signal communication men we still have to the right wing and clarify what the situation is there. The group of houses between Girnen and Brückental should actually still be occupied. If that is not the case, take all the men you can find in the area and seize control of those houses once more as quicky as possible. If this outpost falls, we will not be able to hold Girnen.'

I salute and go to the signal communication men to tell them what is to be done. A few minutes later, we are stomping in a line through the deep snow towards the south-east. The air is misty. Visibility is poor.

After we've gone 200 metres, I see a house in front of us. We spread out and approach carefully. Nothing is impossible in such an unclear situation. Ivan could very well be there.

We go another ten metres and then hear tremendous howling to our left: Stalin's organs! [*TN*: Katyusha rocket launchers]

We rush to the house and dash down the cellar stairs for cover, pressing ourselves to the floor. There are explosions nonstop outside. With the last salvo from the Stalin organ, a piece of shrapnel from a shell casing hits me in the chest. My camouflage jacket is singed. I stand up and am surprised to see that we aren't alone. Several soldiers are crouching on the floor. It seemed that they've completely lost their nerve.

'Who's in command here?' I ask.

A sergeant approaches me. He tells me that he and his men were still in the farmstead ahead of us at noon and had then been forced out by Ivan. Eight men have fallen. The remaining 14 are hunkered down in the cellar we are now in.

'Everybody listen up!' I announce. 'As soon as it gets dark, we will attack and retake the farmstead!'

The sergeant makes a feeble attempt to point out the difficulties of such an undertaking. I look at him. He gives up.

It soon becomes dark.

'Get ready! We will leave the cellar and spread out to the left and right. We will slowly approach the farmstead until we are within 30 metres of it. On my signal, we will storm the farmstead in a single stroke. Once we've managed that, we will push through to the other side of the farmstead and secure the area to the east! Let's go!'

We ascend the stairs. Although it is dark, the snow gives us relatively good visibility. The terrain in front of us offers no cover.

We move forward in a line, step by step with extreme caution. I walk in the middle. The flanks lag back a little. Not a single shot is fired.

If Ivan is allowing us to move forward with the intention of opening fire at the very last moment, we won't stand a chance.

We get to within 60 metres. I can feel the sweat on my forehead. Then it is 40 metres. Then 30. I raise my arm and give the signal to rush forward.

I get to the row of bushes that surround the farmstead in one go. The sergeant is next to me. Silence reigns.

I am horrified to notice that the men haven't rushed forward with me. I leave the bushes and beckon to them to hurry up. Only hesitantly do they come closer.

So much for being ready, I think. This is a new experience for me.

We enter the farmstead in two groups. I go with the group on the right. We carefully move forward in a line along the walls of the house.

A shot rings out behind me. I spin around and see a Russian fall flat on his face. He'd been in a doorway only a few metres behind me. The fusilier behind him comes up to me. 'You were lucky. I only noticed him as he took aim at your back!'

'Thank you!' I said. I can't think of what else to say.

So, it turns out that Ivan is indeed present at the farmstead. We push on to the eastern boundary of the building complex.

Hand grenades explode suddenly on the left side of the farmyard. Submachine guns hammer away in the darkness. That's the sergeant with the other group.

It becomes lively in front of us as well. Ivan is returning fire. I enter a house with a few of my men. We have some degree of cover there. A firefight has broken out in the farmyard. The Russians are only 30 metres away.

The firefight stops. It is remarkably quiet. I peer through the crack in the slightly ajar front door. Nothing can be seen in the inner yard. I cautiously step outside. The men follow.

Ivan has fallen back. He's left his fallen behind. We continue our advance and secure the eastern boundary of the farmstead.

I make it clear to the sergeant that this position is to be held. We check the sentry positions together and brief the men.

I leave three of the signal communication men behind as reinforcements. I make my way back to the battalion with the fourth.

Captain Wolf listens to my report at the command post at 18.40. He then sits down in a corner of the shelter, drafts a written report on the battalion's situation and calls over the signal officer. 'Schneider, you will go up to Girnen, get a vehicle from Staguhn, drive to Division and deliver this report!'

Second Lieutenant Schneider takes the report, goes outside and disappears into the night.

I find some time to pick up my diary to record the day's events. The commander notices this and says: 'Ever since I took command of the battalion, I've seen that you keep your diary up to date with unusual meticulousness. It's none of my business, but what do you hope to achieve by doing this?'

'I've been keeping this diary since 1938 because I think it's important to record the events we're living through, especially from the point of view of the ordinary man. Works on the history of the war will be published in the future. Everyone will be able to read where and when such and such an army was deployed. But I want to record what happened for men like us and how we conducted ourselves in this extraordinary situation. In order to make that possible at some point, I'm writing down the facts and events for each day.'

'And do you think you'll be able to get your records out of East Prussia?' asks Captain Wolf. 'You know what the situation is like.'

'Although the situation is extremely bad, Captain, I am going to assume that I will make it. If I didn't believe this, I would give up. But I will not give up!'

The commander nods and then turns away without saying another word. I suspect I haven't convinced him.

20 January: It is a relatively quiet night. Soviet artillery fires on Girnen every now and then.

The noise of battle can be heard outside when I wake up. I glance at the clock. 0700 hours! It is still dark. The commander reaches for the field telephone. Nothing! The connection is broken.

A messenger arrives from the 3rd Company. 'Captain, Ivan was in our trench! We hurled him back with a counter-thrust. We suffered heavy losses. The company commander says that we cannot repel further attacks without reinforcements.'

The battalion commander picks up his submachine gun. 'Take me to the 3rd Company. I want to see what's going on there.'

It is now daylight. The machine-gun fire across the front of the battalion is getting closer and increasing in intensity. We have no idea what the situation is for the neighbouring formations. We can't see them from where we are.

The commander returns at noon. 'The companies repelled four attacks of battalion strength this morning. It is highly unlikely that further attacks can be intercepted. You are aware that the 1st Company is completely out of the picture. The combat strength of the other companies has been reduced to an absolute minimum. At nightfall, we will fall back to the range of hills to the north-west of Girnen. You will see to it that all documents here at the headquarters are destroyed. You are responsible for ensuring that nothing falls into Ivan's hands.'

Captain Wolf goes outside again to visit the companies.

The company sergeant major from the supply company arrives with rations and ammunition. To my great surprise, he also has a letter for me. I tear open the envelope. Inside is a hastily written note with a letter that I'd sent to Jupp Reinardy at the beginning of December 1944. Hands shaking, I read the note. It says that

Second Lieutenant Reinardy was shot down over Krakow on 26 December and that for this reason my letter has been sent back. The signature is illegible. The world stands still for a moment. Jupp Reinardy is dead. If he is dead, then so too are Gert Siller and Franz Felician.

It is only much later that I find out that my old crew together with Squadron Leader (Major) Badorrek, a recipient of the Knight's Cross of the Iron Cross with Oak Leaves and the commander of the 3. Ergänzungs-Fernaufklärungsgruppe (3rd Long-Range Reconnaissance Group), hadn't survived. They had taken off from Stubendorf Officer Training School and had been shot down by American P-51 Mustang long-range fighters in the vicinity of Krakow. I feel empty inside and go into the shelter with a heavy heart.

Impacts near the entrance of the command post bring me back to the present. Two of my men are carrying the headquarters documents outside. I set fire to the pile of paper and instruct the fusiliers to see to it that it all burns properly.

I look up at the sound of a vehicle approaching. A Volkswagen command car has emerged from the depression behind our shelter. The car stops. An officer gets out. As he comes closer, I recognise him as Major Sandrock, the commander of the Sturmgeschützabteilung 2 'Hermann Göring' (2nd Assault Gun Battalion 'Hermann Göring').

I walk towards the major and salute. He points to the blazing fire. 'What are you doing there?'

'Major, I have orders to destroy all our documents. We will be falling back to a position to the north of Girnen at nightfall!'

'You put it very elegantly. In your situation, "falling back" means nothing other than "retreating", or do you seriously believe that you will reoccupy this position at some point? I hope you are aware that this measure is not in the interests of the division!'

'Major, I am carrying out my orders here. I will inform my commander of your concerns as soon as he returns from the front.'

Major Sandrock says no more. He salutes and drives off. I have no doubt that Division HQ will soon know that the fusilier battalion will be moving its positions 500 metres to the west.

At 1600 hours, I point out the house on the slope behind us to the battalion messengers. 'Go back and occupy the house over there. I will follow in a quarter of an hour.'

Captain Wolf returns from the front. I report Major Sandrock's visit to him.

The commander doesn't comment on that at all. Instead, he says: 'Please give me your Iron Cross, First Class. I need it as an award on the battlefield for a corporal from the 2nd Company.'

I know that Captain Wolf already used his own Iron Cross for a similar purpose yesterday. He continues: 'Without the perseverance of this corporal at the machine gun, his company would have been lost, and so too most likely would we have been. He continued to fire at the advancing Russians even though his comrades in his machine-gun team had fallen and his position had been surrounded. Elements of his company managed to get out in a counter-push. Now, you will go back to the new position. I will be there in an hour.'

The terrain between the command post and the Girnen–Husarenberg road slopes slightly downwards. I can't be seen by the enemy from there. I then go up the slope on the other side of the road. The gradient is so steep that I make only slow progress.

I am halfway up when the Russians notice me. There is mortar fire. I hurl myself into the wet snow and wait.

After a few minutes, I jump up and continue to make my way up the slope. There is more mortar fire. I take cover again. It takes me 40 minutes to cover 250 metres.

Utterly exhausted, I reach the top of the hill. Up here is the road that leads from Girnen to the north over Mount Husaren (Hill 121.8) to Plicken.

I glance back at the lower-lying ground that we've defended thus far at so great a cost and wonder why we didn't occupied the hill I now stand on from the outset. There is a wide field of fire from here. It is much easier to resist an advancing enemy from high ground.

We are now at a small farmstead. The cellar has been reinforced and is supported with beams. The pioneer troops of Captain Böttcher's Fallschirm-Panzerpionierbataillon 2 'Hermann Göring' (2nd Parachute Panzer Pioneer Battalion 'Hermann Göring') have done solid work.

The trenches in front of the command post are full of snow.

The commander arrives with the remnants of the companies at 1800 hours. The distribution of the troops to their positions proceeds quickly.

I write down the details of the new situation in a report. Captain Wolf signs it, and Second Lieutenant Schneider sets off to deliver it to Division.

The commander lies down to get some sleep at 2100 hours. It was only this afternoon that I'd noticed for the first time that the constant strain has even taken its toll on him.

A divisional orderly officer comes down the steps into our cellar at 22.30. 'I want to speak to the commander!'

'Do me a favour and let the commander get his sleep,' I said. 'We need him to be reasonably refreshed when all hell breaks loose again tomorrow.'

'Mr Knoblauch, you will be held responsible if anything goes wrong here. The division is retreating tonight. I have the express order to inform the commander personally of the withdrawal movement.'

I don't budge. 'Let Captain Wolf sleep.'

'Very well. You will sign what I am now passing on to you and what was intended for your commander. At 0100 hours, the fusilier battalion will leave its current position and will retreat via Alt Wusterwitz, Schulzenwalde, Bahnfelde (Jucknischken), Wildhorst (Schakumehlen) and Angerhöh (Szuskehmen) so that, by 0600 hours, it can move into the new position that has been prepared on the bank of the Angerapp in the vicinity of Angermühle. You will be supplied with more mortar ammunition in Karlswald Forest. Schulzenwalde is to be held until 0400 hours, and the rail and road junction at Bahnfelde is to be defended until 0600 hours. The withdrawal will be carried out in silence. No fire. No explosions.'

I take notes and mark the route of retreat and the new position on the Angerapp on my map. I sign in the absence of the commander and the orderly officer goes to leave. He turns halfway up the steps. 'You knew First Lieutenant Planert from the 3rd Regiment. He was killed in action a few days ago.'

Captain Wolf sleeps. I consider that's a good thing and prepare the battalion order for the withdrawal. Then the messengers are dispatched to the companies.

The commander stirs at 23.10 and is soon on his feet. 'Anything to report, Knoblauch?'

'Yes, Captain! The battalion is to retreat to the Angerapp line at Angermühle. The divisional order was delivered by the orderly officer at 22.30. I took the liberty of issuing a corresponding order to the companies.'

'Show me the order,' says Captain Wolf. He reads it and hands it back to me. 'You will drive to Angermühle immediately and set up the command post. The bulk of the battalion will probably reach Angerhöh by 0500 hours. The rearguard platoon will establish contact with the battalion at sunrise. See to it that the troops know where they are supposed to go from the road fork on the northern outskirts of Angerhöh.'

I am dismissed. I call my driver, and off we go through the night in the direction of Alt Wusterwitz.

21 January: The wind carries only a faint sound of battle over to us from the front behind us.

It is difficult to find our way in the dark. If we get stuck in the snow the consequences will dire. The streets and roads are empty. I wonder what routes the other battalions are taking as the carry out their withdrawal. Or are there no longer any other battalions in this sector?

After getting lost for a short time near Alt Wusterwitz, we reach the railway crossing in Bahnfelde at 00.35. I hope the rearguard platoon will manage to bring the Russians to a halt there.

We get stuck in a snowdrift a short distance beyond Wildhorst. I get out. It takes us 20 minutes to get going again.

The outlines of houses appear in the darkness ahead of us at 0100 hours. A snow-encrusted town sign stands to the right side of the road.

I have us come to a stop. I scrape the snow off the sign with the butt of my submachine gun. It read: Angerhöh.

We drive on. A large courtyard lies to the right of the road, probably belonging to an estate. The place is empty. We turn to the right in the middle of the village and, after 400 metres, reach the fork in the road on the northern outskirts. This is where I will see to the distribution of the forces of the battalion in a few hours' time.

I direct the driver to take the left fork in the road. After another 800 metres, we cross the Angerapp at Angermühle.

The mill buildings are located directly next to the bridge on the right-hand side of the road on the west bank of the Angerapp. I order the driver to stop. Holding my torch, I go into the rooms of the mill. It isn't particularly inviting, but it is still better than not having a roof over our heads. It will still be a few hours before the arrival of the battalion.

The driver and I make use of the time to inspect the positions. The trenches lie along the upper part of the steep bank of the Angerapp. Tunnels have been dug into the bluff banks. The whole thing looks quite extensive. Compared to what we've had thus far, the Angerapp line is a princely estate.

German soldiers defended the Fatherland against the advancing regiments of the tsar during World War I. They did so with some degree of success. By contrast, we are now in a hopeless situation in our fight against the mass of the Red Army.

I drive out to the fork in the road in good time. It is 05.20. The spearhead of the battalion appears in Angerhöh, and soon afterwards the commander's car rolls up. 'How do the positions look, Knoblauch?'

'The positions are in good shape, Captain! Good field of fire and solid shelters!'

I drive up to the positions with the commander. He looks around and nods in satisfaction. The battalion is now approaching us in a line out of the darkness. The men move into their positions and ready themselves. How much time we still have depends on whether the rearguard platoon will be able bring Ivan to a halt.

The commander turns to me. 'I will take care of the occupation of the positions. You will go back to Angerhöh and be ready for the rearguard platoon when it arrives. You'll find me in the mill on the other side of the Angerapp.'

I drive back to Angerhöh and wait at the eastern exit of the village. Time passes slowly. The driver and I walk up and down the road. Both of us are freezing. It is only with the utmost effort and feeling of responsibility that I don't sit down in the car and go to sleep. I can't fool myself any longer. I am physically exhausted!

The deceptive silence is broken by machine-gun fire at 05.55. I listen into the night. It is probably near Bahnfelde. With any luck the rearguard platoon will be able to disengage from the enemy in time.

'Is there anything to eat, First Lieutenant?'

It is the first time I've been asked this. 'No, there isn't. But I have a packet of cigarettes. You can have one if you'd like.'

He takes the packet and goes behind a house wall to light a cigarette.

It is still dark at 07.40. Figures appear on the snow-covered road and approach us slowly.

Is that our rearguard platoon or the Russian infantry spearhead? I call out to the driver: 'Start the engine! If that is Ivan, we'll drive off at full speed!'

Taking cover at the corner of a house, I call out to the approaching figures: 'Who goes there?'

'Fusilier battalion!' comes the reply.

I go to meet the men. The platoon leader delivers his report. 'Ivan pursued us only hesitantly towards Schulzenwalde. We were able to withdraw without contact with the enemy. Then there was a fierce firefight at Bahnfelde. Only with great effort did the platoon disengage. It wasn't possible to fall back via Wildhorst (Schakumehlen). So that we wouldn't be cut off, we first went back along the road to Dingelau (Glasgirren) and then marched rapidly to Angerhöh via Gudwainen.'

The men of the rearguard platoon stand round me. Their faces show what they've been through. Some of them are barely able to stand on their own feet.

The platoon leader speaks again. 'We shouldn't stay here. Ivan is only a few minutes behind us!'

I see to it that the machine guns and ammunition boxes are loaded into the Volkswagen and then go with the men of the rearguard platoon in the direction of Angermühle.

It is now 0800 hours. The sun shines through the morning haze above Karlswald Forest.

We reach the positions on the east bank of the Angerapp. While I am briefing the men, machine-gun fire is suddenly heard from the direction of Wiekmünde. Something seems to hit my stomach as I stand on the edge of the trench. It's as if I've been kicked by a horse, and I fall into the trench behind me.

I am astonished to discover that I'm not wounded. A bullet has gone through my dispatch case and has lodged itself in a packet of letters.

More troops retreat along the road near Angermühle throughout the morning. They are badly battered formations without heavy weaponry. The troops look just as run down as we were.

Artillery fire commences at noon. The commander, having correctly assessed the situation, has in the meantime moved the command post to one of the tunnels in the steep bank of the Angerapp.

Our positions are so well constructed that we can look forward to the coming days with confidence.

The order for the next withdrawal movement arrives in the afternoon. We are extremely disappointed. If a position like this one here at the Angerapp has to be abandoned without a fight, the overall situation must be particularly bad.

But who among us can know that? We don't even know what's going on 1,000 metres to our north or south.

After nightfall, I drive to Gross Datzen via Kieselheim and Grosspreussenbruch. I cross the Angerapp–Insterburg railway line to the east of Königsgarten and come to the village of Ballethen after another five kilometres.

We aren't alone here. A 7.5cm anti-tank gun has been positioned on the outskirts of the village. We are glad to see it there.

It takes a few hours for the battalion to arrive and move into position. To our left are elements of the 4. Regiment 'Hermann Göring'. Ivan is pursuing us quickly. He seeks to infiltrate Ballethen this very evening, but we manage to repel him.

22 January: At 0200 hours we hear our MG 42 machine gun firing away from its position on the road to Köskeim. The commander wakes up immediately and goes outside with a messenger. The rest of the staff prepare for all-round defence.

I cautiously step out into the night with my men. We are still near the front door when we are subjected to submachine-gun fire. We have a group of Russians in front of us who are shooting wildly. They are only 15 metres away.

I drop behind a garden fence and open fire on the figures who, despite the darkness, stand out against the snow. I can see the muzzle flashes from the weapons of my men all around me. Then it goes quiet. Silence set in after the last hand grenade detonated. It is a deathly silence.

There is a fusilier who's crumpled to the ground by the front door. He is dead. A burst of submachine-gun fire has torn open his chest. None of the Russians have survived.

The firing in the entire area comes to a stop at 0300 hours. Ivan must have suffered heavy casualties in front of our positions.

He tries again shortly before daybreak and once more runs into the fire of the fusilier troops. Five men of the battalion fall in action.

The hours creep by slowly. Everyone feels our situation is hopeless. But no one says anything about it. I find myself trying to guess what I'll do when the last shot is finally fired and Ivan is standing at the front door. I don't dare dwell on the thought of captivity.

Surprisingly, the commander of the supply company arrives in a truck. He delivers rations and ammunition.

It has become dark again. Apart from a few sentries, the men have slept during the day. Now the greatest vigilance is required.

Artillery fire can be heard to our north-west. It might be to the west of Insterburg. Flares hang in the sky above our positions.

23 January: There is a sudden intense exchange of fire at 02.20. We rush outside.

The advancing Russian forces are easily recognisable on the snow-covered surface and in the dim light provided by the flares. Our machine guns hammer away at them incessantly.

This nightmare lasts almost 20 minutes. Then the enemy's bellowing becomes fainter and finally stops. Silence reigns. Two of our men have been wounded. A Russian cries out from the area beyond the front. He is whimpering a few minutes later, and then the easterly wind sweeps away the last of his noise. I shiver.

Only a few months ago we were still making the effort to recover wounded Russians if they were lying in the area immediately in front of our positions. But we stopped doing that after the Red Army soldiers thought it acceptable to lure our men into a deadly trap with deceptive cries of pain. The brutality of this conflict has reached new levels.

The Russians try again before sunrise. The attackers collapse, fatally wounded, 20 metres from our positions. Only a few of them manage to withdraw into the darkness.

It seems to me that there is now a decrease in the persistence of the attacks. The enemy is presumably attempting to determine whether we will make a serious effort to hold on to this position or whether we will simply leave rearguards behind while we fall back.

Time passes slowly. Eventually, at 1800 hours, the order arrives for the retreat to the Masurian fortifications. For the fusilier troops, this will mean a 38-kilometre march on foot along bad roads and through wet snow with Ivan breathing down their necks.

I drive ahead with two messengers in order to scout out the new position to the north of Nordenburg. The companies disengage silently a short time later and set off for the west.

We drive into the darkness. I order us to stop after eight kilometres. I'm not sure whether we are on the right track. We drove through the village of

Trempen ten minutes ago. I look at the map with my flashlight. Ernstburg ought to be ahead.

We drive on. Ernstburg is nowhere in sight. I give it another five minutes and then get us to stop again. A couple of barns stand to our left. They might be part of an outlying estate, but where are we exactly?

I lost my prismatic compass last night in the firefight with the Russians in Ballethen. The sky is overcast, so I won't be able to orient myself by the stars. The road is unoccupied, so there is no one to ask. There is the noise of battle to be heard in the distance, so that direction has to be towards the east.

I rotate my map this way and that and decided that we'll have to drive further. We can't spend the winter where we are.

The road leads through a snow-covered forest. There isn't a soul in sight.

I call a halt once more and get out to examine the road surface. There are fresh tracks. We drive off again and, after half an hour, cross a railway line.

24 January: It is well after midnight. We come across a village. In the middle of the village, I notice a faint glow of light behind a poorly covered window. We come to a stop.

My men remain in the vehicle with the engine running. I walk towards the house and enter cautiously, my finger on the trigger of my P38.

I'm pleasantly surprised by what I see. Inside is a detail of the Fallschirm-Panzerartillerieregiment 2 'Hermann Göring'. In charge is a captain who I met during the divisional map exercise. The artillerymen look just as unkempt and run down as I do.

I see a pot on the stove containing a hot beverage. My eyes are drawn to it. The captain notices this and invites me to help myself.

'Thank you very much, Captain. Two of my men are outside. I'm sure you wouldn't mind if they could …?'

'Certainly. Bring them in!'

We sip tea that the residents of this house left behind when they fled from the Russians. There is no sugar.

'So,' said the captain, 'what are you doing in this damned part of the country?'

'I could ask you the same thing, Captain! I'll be honest: I've totally lost my way. I have no idea which way is forward or back!'

'That's quite funny, my dear fellow! I seem to remember that you were an airman. Long-range reconnaissance? I hope you'll forgive me, but I'm pleased to hear that even reconnaissance airmen can sometimes lose their bearings!'

'Unfortunately, it's not so funny for me. I would be grateful if you could show me on the map where we are.'

I make a rough estimate as to how long it will take for the battalion to reach the Masurian fortifications. I decide that I can allow myself and my men another 30 minutes to rest in the warmth of this house.

Once that time has passed, we say goodbye to the artillerymen and go back outside. The captain accompanies us to the front door and says: 'By the way, are you aware that Ivan has already pushed beyond Insterburg? Everything seems to be in a state of disorder. Keep your chin up. Good luck!'

'Thank you very much, Captain. We're all in need of luck.'

An icy wind is blowing towards us, and light snowfall has started. We still have a good 12 kilometres in front of us as the crow flies.

Ten minutes pass. Again I feel that we've gone the wrong way. It is enough to drive anyone to despair.

I order that we come to a halt and turn off the engine. We listen to the night. I think I can hear engine sounds in the distance, slightly to the left. I decide that we will drive on in the direction of these noises.

The road we're driving on is in poor condition. Our progress is slow.

Another half an hour goes by. Ahead is a large road which runs perpendicular to our road. We approach it carefully. All kinds of vehicles are rolling along it. They are German.

I go up to a truck that has stopped and speak to the driver. 'Tell me, where does this road lead?'

He looks at me suspiciously and says: 'I don't know where the road leads. I only know that we came from Angerapp.'

That answer satisfies me. We are on the road that runs west from Angerapp and that meets Reichsstrasse 139 to the north of Nordenburg, near Pentlack.

We join the travelling column and continue west. We reach Reichsstrasse 139 after half an hour, turn left and drive into Pentlack. A farmstead lies to the right of the road. We turn right out of the column and reach the Plattau estate via Bruchort. It is here, in accordance with the commander's orders, that I will set up the command post.

We drive into the estate. I get out of the car and approach the buildings with my men. I notice that a light is on in the outbuilding. We go inside. Two soldiers from another unit are standing in front of a large table on which several food canisters have been placed. They are just about to leave.

My men go closer and look at the contents of the canisters. I am also curious.

The canisters are full to the brim with roasted goose drumsticks. It is apparent that all the geese on the estate have been slaughtered here. I decide I'd try to take some for me and my men.

The German main line of resistance along the Weidengrund–Hochfliess road under fire from Soviet artillery in October 1944.

A bridge built by pioneer troops across the Rominte near Hochfliess. A shortage of tractors meant that trucks had to tow the 8.8cm anti-aircraft guns.

A Soviet aircraft, presumably an Il-2, shot down in the vicinity of Gumbinnen.

A Soviet anti-aircraft gun position that has been taken in a German counter-thrust in October 1944.

First Lieutenant Karl Rossmann led the 16th Company of Flakregiment (mot.) (Motorised Flak Regiment) 'Hermann Göring' and, later as a major, the Fallschirm-Panzerregiment 1 'Hermann Göring'.

Major Hans Sandrock, commander of the Sturmgeschützabteilung 2 (2nd Assault Gun Battalion) 'Hermann Göring'.

Major Heinz-Hubert Schwein, first general staff officer of the Fallschirm-Panzergrenadierdivision 2 'Hermann Göring'.

Colonel, and later Brigadier, Erich Walther, commander of the Fallschirm-Panzergrenadierdivision 2 'Hermann Göring'. He died of starvation on 26 December 1948 in the Soviet Buchenwald concentration camp.

Colonel Paul Conrath (holding the map), commander of Flakregiment (mot.) 'Hermann Göring'. Later, as a brigadier, he was the commander of Panzerdivision 'Hermann Göring'.

Major Constantin Hahm, commander of the II Battalion of Fallschirm-Panzerregiment 'Hermann Göring'.

Colonel Waldemar Kluge, commander of the Fallschirm-Panzergrenadierregiment 4 'Hermann Göring'.

Autumn 1944: a company of German soldiers marches through Gumbinnen.

The Bismack tower to the west of the Plicken Hills was blown up on 21 January 1945 by the 14th Pioneer Company of the Fallschirm-Panzergrenadierregiment 4 'Hermann Göring'.

Town sign for Gumbinnen in East Prussia in autumn 1944.

The 8.8cm anti-aircraft gun was a highly effective weapon against targets on the ground and in the air until the end of the war.

When fired from its wheels, the 8.8cm anti-aircraft gun was not quite so accurate as it was when completely emplaced, but that was the way it was used if the situation demanded it.

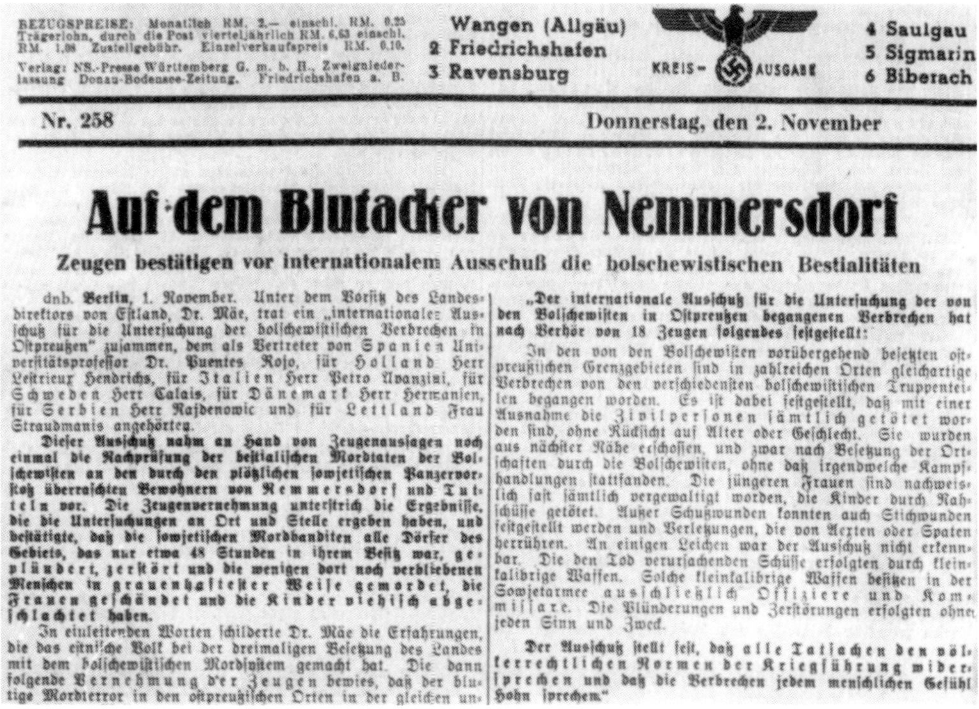

BEZUGSPREISE: Monatlich RM. 2.— einschl. RM. 0.25 Trägerlohn, durch die Post vierteljährlich RM. 6.63 einschl. RM. 1.08 Zustellgebühr. Einzelverkaufspreis RM. 0.10.
Verlag: NS.-Presse Württemberg G. m. b. H., Zweigniederlassung Donau-Bodensee-Zeitung. Friedrichshafen a. B.

Wangen (Allgäu)
2 Friedrichshafen
3 Ravensburg

4 Saulgau
5 Sigmarin
6 Biberach

Nr. 258   Donnerstag, den 2. November

Auf dem Blutacker von Nemmersdorf

Zeugen bestätigen vor internationalem Ausschuß die bolschewistischen Bestialitäten

dnb. Berlin, 1. November. Unter dem Vorsitz des Landesdirektors von Estland, Dr. Mäe, trat ein „internationaler Ausschuß für die Untersuchung der bolschewistischen Verbrechen in Ostpreußen" zusammen, dem als Vertreter von Spanien Universitätsprofessor Dr. Puentes Rojo, für Holland Herr Leitrieur Hendrichs, für Italien Herr Petro Avanzini, für Schweden Herr Calais, für Dänemark Herr Hermanien, für Serbien Herr Rajdenowic und für Lettland Frau Straudmanis angehörten.

Dieser Ausschuß nahm an Hand von Zeugenaussagen noch einmal die Nachprüfung der bestialischen Mordtaten der Bolschewisten an den durch den plötzlichen sowjetischen Panzervorstoß überraschten Bewohnern von Nemmersdorf und Tuteln vor. Die Zeugenvernehmung unterstrich die Ergebnisse, die die Untersuchungen an Ort und Stelle ergeben haben, und bestätigte, daß die sowjetischen Mordbanditen alle Dörfer des Gebiets, das nur etwa 48 Stunden in ihrem Besitz war, geplündert, zerstört und die wenigen dort noch verbliebenen Menschen in grauenhaftester Weise gemordet, die Frauen geschändet und die Kinder viehisch abgeschlachtet haben.

In einleitenden Worten schilderte Dr. Mäe die Erfahrungen, die das estnische Volk bei der dreimaligen Besetzung des Landes mit dem bolschewistischen Mordsystem gemacht hat. Die dann folgende Vernehmung der Zeugen bewies, daß der blutige Mordterror in den ostpreußischen Orten in der gleichen un-

„Der internationale Ausschuß für die Untersuchung der von den Bolschewisten in Ostpreußen begangenen Verbrechen hat nach Verhör von 18 Zeugen folgendes festgestellt:

In den von den Bolschewisten vorübergehend besetzten ostpreußischen Grenzgebieten sind in zahlreichen Orten gleichartige Verbrechen von den verschiedensten bolschewistischen Truppenteilen begangen worden. Es ist dabei festgestellt, daß mit einer Ausnahme die Zivilpersonen sämtlich getötet worden sind, ohne Rücksicht auf Alter oder Geschlecht. Sie wurden aus nächster Nähe erschossen, und zwar nach Besetzung der Ortschaften durch die Bolschewisten, ohne daß irgendwelche Kampfhandlungen stattfanden. Die jüngeren Frauen sind nachweislich fast sämtlich vergewaltigt worden, die Kinder durch Nahschüsse getötet. Außer Schußwunden konnten auch Stichwunden festgestellt werden und Verletzungen, die von Äxten oder Spaten herrühren. An einigen Leichen war der Ausschuß nicht erkennbar. Die den Tod verursachenden Schüsse erfolgten durch kleinkalibrige Waffen. Solche kleinkalibrige Waffen besitzen in der Sowjetarmee ausschließlich Offiziere und Kommissare. Die Plünderungen und Zerstörungen erfolgten ohne jeden Sinn und Zweck.

Der Ausschuß stellt fest, daß alle Tatsachen den völkerrechtlichen Normen der Kriegführung widersprechen und daß die Verbrechen jedem menschlichen Gefühl Hohn sprechen."

A National Socialist article about Soviet atrocities in East Prussia in 1944. International investigations were in fact carried out, but the outcome of the war meant there was never any atonement.

A four-barrelled 2cm anti-aircraft gun at Gertenau in autumn 1944.

A disabled T-34 in the trench before Nemmersdorf on 23 October 1944.

This heavy Stalin tank was hit near Hochfliess in January 1945.

This T-34 toppled over as the bridge across the Angerapp near Nemmersdorf was blown up.

A burned-out T-34-85 near Husarenberg.

The Fallschirm-Panzerfüsilierbataillon 2 'Hermann Göring' in the Girnen position to the south-south-east of Gumbinnen from 17 December 1944 until 20 January 1945.

A composite aerial photograph of Girnen in 1944.

Reichsstrasse 138, Ohldorf–Samfelde.

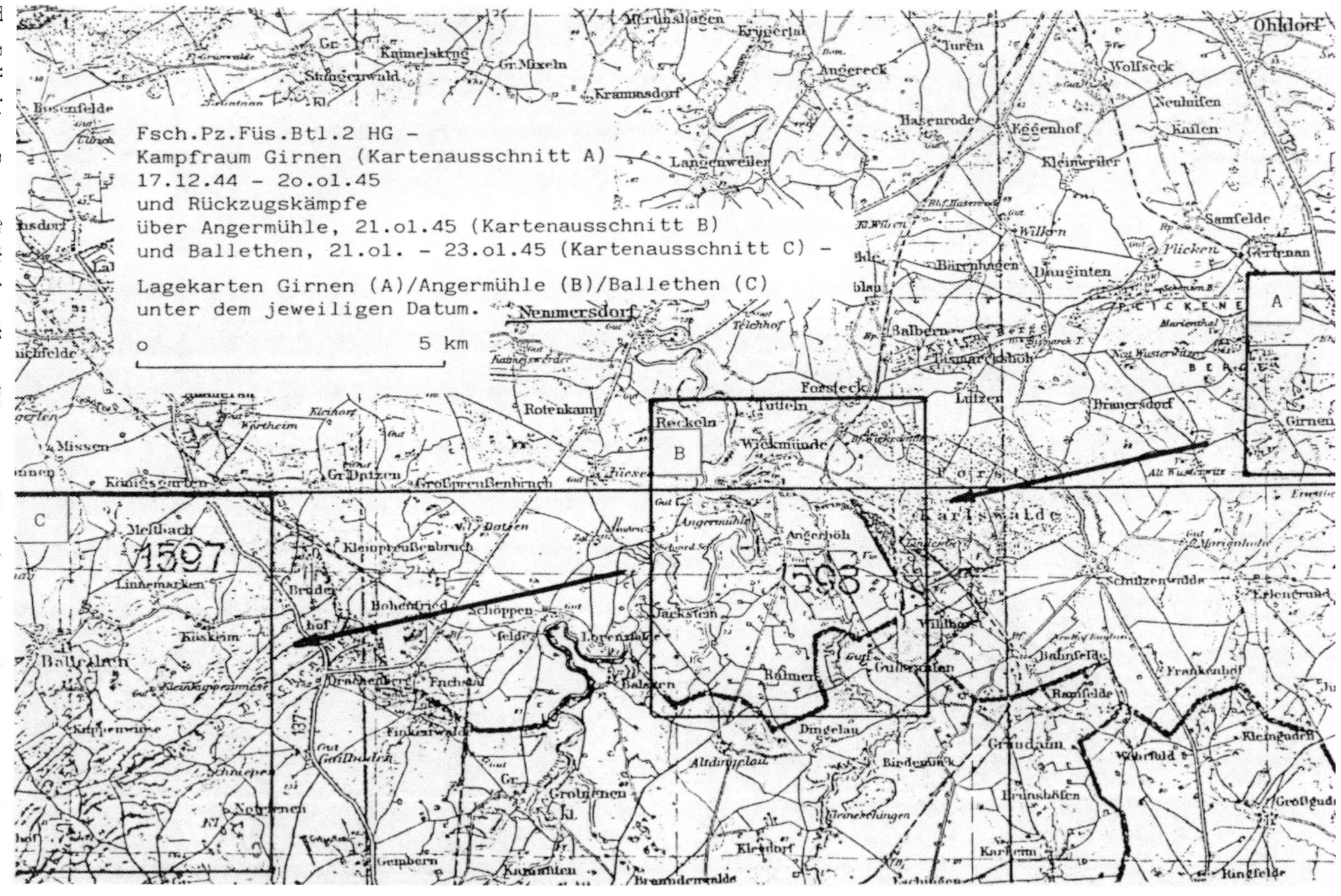

The Fallschirm-Panzerfüsilierbataillon 2 'Hermann Göring' in the combat zone around Girnen and in the withdrawal battles through Angermühle and Ballethen.

A 7.5cm PaK 40 in the defensive combat in East Prussia in January 1945.

A Panther tank of the 'Hermann Göring' troops taking part in a counter-thrust.

Armoured personnel carriers of the 'Hermann Göring' panzer grenadier troops near Friedland in January 1945.

A StuG III G in the sector of the Fallschirm-Panzerfüsilierbataillon 2 'Hermann Göring' near Girnen on 20 January 1945.

First Lieutenant Knoblauch in front of the command post of the Fallschirm-Panzerfüsilierbataillon 2 'Hermann Göring' in January 1945.

In front of the command post of the Fallschirm-Panzerfüsilierbataillon 2 'Hermann Göring' in the Girnen position in December 1944 are, from left, First Lieutenant Knoblauch (battalion adjutant), Second Lieutenant Küchel (orderly officer), Captain Wolf (battalion commander) and First Lieutenant Kalff (commander of the 3rd Company).

First Lieutenant Karl Knoblauch just before the major Soviet winter offensive commenced on 12 January 1945.

Karl Knoblauch maintained his sense of humour even in difficult times.

Karl Knoblauch in front of the command post of the Fallschirm-Panzerfüsilierbataillon 2 'Hermann Göring' the day before the Soviet winter offensive of 12 January 1945.

An older corporal thinks I'm being presumptuous. 'That's not for you! Get out of here!'

My men quickly intervene. 'Shall we make mincemeat out of him, First Lieutenant?'

The corporal goes pale. He hadn't thought I was an officer. My rank insignia is hidden beneath my camouflage jacket.

I remain calm and come to a decision. 'Of the ten canisters, one will stay here. Take the rest. And keep a low profile.'

The soldiers get moving. They have to go back and forth several times to load the canisters into the vehicle.

It is 05.30. I drive with my men to the forest east of the estate. We get out and walk through snow-covered paths to the other edge of the forest. There are supposed to be dug-out positions there.

It is soon 06.20. Our search for the positions has thus far been in vain. If I can't find them before the arrival of the battalion, there'll be serious trouble.

I decide to go south along the eastern edge of the forest, in the direction of the Bruchort forester's lodge. After about 100 metres, I come across three men crouching in a snow pit with a machine gun. I approach them and ask: 'Who are you?'

'We are from the Volkssturm and are to hold this position until regular troops arrive. There are 40 men here at the edge of the forest who are waiting to be relieved.'

'You're in luck. The regular troops will be here in an hour. Now tell me about that strange machine gun you have there.'

'This is a Belgian machine gun. Unfortunately, we don't have any Belgian ammunition.'

I am speechless for a moment and then bid them farewell. The two men behind me are discussing what they've just heard. One of them says, 'Whoever is responsible for this should be court-martialled. These old men with their pitiful weaponry stand no chance against Ivan.'

The spearhead of the battalion appears on its way from Pentlack at 07.10. It is led by a master sergeant, and the men follow in a line. I enquire about the commander.

'Captain Wolf is walking or driving at the rear of the battalion. I estimate he will be here in 20 minutes.'

The men who traipse past me are at the end of their tether. Their faces are expressionless. None of them says a word. Each man apathetically follows in the footsteps of the one in front.

I assign the master sergeant one of my men so that the positions at the edge of the forest can be occupied without losing any time.

The next company, or what is left of it, goes past. The picture is the same. They are the same exhausted figures.

The commander's car churns through the snow and comes to a halt nearby. 'Knoblauch, where are the prepared positions?'

'The positions lie along the edge of the forest, Captain, but they've hardly been prepared. The trenches are covered in snow. Some old men from the Volkssturm are crouched in the snow pits and are waiting for us to relieve them.'

'Instruct the rest of the battalion where to go and send the Volkssturm troops home. I don't want to be responsible for them. I will drive to the Plattau estate now and will expect you there once the last man is in position. Speed is of the essence. Ivan will be here in half an hour at the latest!'

The conditions in the positions are catastrophic. The deep trenches are full of snow and difficult to locate. I speak with the company commanders and explain to them where the battalion command post is to be found.

The sun rises by 0800 hours, but it doesn't shine through the low clouds. I am on the left wing of the battalion, which is where the forest lies only 150 metres from the road connecting Pentlack and Klein Gnie. That road runs parallel to the main line of resistance, and on the other side is the Klein Pentlack forester's lodge.

'Take cover!' a soldier calls out to me. 'Ivan is over there in the roadside ditch!'

I drop to the ground at once. A glance through the binoculars reveals that at least 100 men have taken up positions opposite us.

I am convinced that our companies are ready for battle. The machine guns are manned. The remaining troops are making use of the opportunity to sleep. Accompanied by a messenger, I go back through the snowy forest to the Plattau estate.

We have no heavy weaponry whatsoever. We don't even have the anti-tank gun that had reinforced our position in Ballethen. That was the gun that put out of action a Soviet scout car that had been approaching us at high speed. I will never forget that incident. The scout car was hit by the very first shell at a distance of 80 metres! It split open like a tin can. Two wheels rolled towards us across the snow from the burning wreckage. The crew ascended to heaven with the rising plume of smoke.

The commander is keeping busy. The supply company will be bringing warm rations at nightfall. I expect this will help improve morale.

Captain Wolf turns to me. 'The party man responsible for the Volkssturm troops here left a few minutes ago. I suggested to him that he go as far back as possible with his inadequately equipped men. You know, I really feel sorry for this man, the poor wretch. The future looks bad, but he still believes we'll be able to hold on to East Prussia. If Ivan catches him in his uniform, he'll be done for! Anyway,

I don't particularly like the fact that the command post is so far away, but we can't set it up in the forest. I'd have no influence on the course of events there. The signal communication men are currently laying the cables to the companies.'

I think of the totally exhausted men in the trenches at the front and I'm glad that the principle of order and obedience is still intact at all levels.

The sound of battle intensifies. We can hear the firing of our MG 42 machine gun at the edge of the forest opposite the Pentlack forester's lodge. And then the first mortar shells explode nearby in the estate. The windowpanes shatter, and plaster falls from the ceiling.

The commander has gone to visit our positions at the front. Heavy artillery fire can be heard to our north. It might be in the vicinity of Hochlindenberg, two kilometres away. I look at my map. The terrain between the Plattau estate and Hochlindenberg is unoccupied. If Ivan were to infiltrate the front there, he'd soon be to our rear. There is no way for us to prevent that.

Captain Wolf returns from the front at 15.50, and an orderly officer arrives shortly afterwards. The battalion adjutants are to visit the division at 16.30 to receive new orders.

I fetch my map-mounting board and call the driver. We get into the command car and wait in the cover of a barn wall. Once there is a pause in the firing, the driver puts the car into gear and puts his foot down. We shoot out of the estate like a rocket and onto the road to Ellernbruch.

It is dark now. The Russian mortar fire lies behind us. Only slowly do we make progress on the snow-covered roads.

After 20 minutes, I am no longer certain if we are going the right way. After another five minutes, I am sure we are lost. I get us to turn around. We drive back and start again.

I have us come to a halt a short distance from Neusobrost so that I can have another look at my map in the dim illumination of my flashlight. My gaze drifts by chance to the snowy surface. To my right, I see figures moving slowly westwards through the evening mist. Russians? I hesitate at first, but then I recognise the round winter hats and the long coats. The Red Army soldiers are only 40 or 50 metres away. There is also movement in the area to our left. We've got ourselves in the middle of a company that is advancing to the west on either side of the road.

I tell my driver to proceed carefully. I only hope that we don't get stuck. Only once we have made it past Neusobrost do we breathe a sigh of relief.

It is late. The meeting at the divisional headquarters will have begun without me.

I finally arrive there at 17.10. The farmstead looks deserted.

I get out of the command car and approach the guard who stands in front of the staff quarters. 'Where can I find the first general staff officer?'

'Just go in. The meeting's already over.'

I bump into Major Schweim in the hallway. He manages to recognise me in the dim candlelight. 'Knoblauch, where've you been?'

'Apologies, Major, I lost my way.'

The major leads me through a door, where I then stand in front of the divisional commander, Colonel Walther.

I report and inform him of the Russians who've infiltrated the front east of Neusobrost. The colonel doesn't react to this news. He says drily: 'From now on the fusilier battalion is subordinate to the 21. Infanteriedivision, specifically the Grenadierregiment 45. The regiment will establish communication with you. Your sector will be expanded to the north and south by 500 metres. Inform your commander and see to it that everything that needs to be done is carried out. What is the strength of your battalion?'

'The light companies had a strength of approximately 20 men each this morning, and the heavy approximately 35 men.'

The colonel glances at his first general staff officer and then shakes my hand. 'It could be that the Russians have already blocked your way back. If that is the case, leave your car and try to get to your battalion on foot. Explain the new situation to your driver, especially about being placed under the command of Grenadierregiment 45. One of you needs to make it back!'

It seems to me that the colonel is proceeding on the assumption that the fusilier battalion is going to be annihilated at its current position.

I get into the Volkswagen, the driver starts the engine, and the return journey begins.

Going back via Neusobrost seems hopeless to me. I think it better to take the route via Gross Sobrost and Waldeck despite the fact that it is covered in deep snow and hasn't been used for a long time.

We drive on at walking pace. We don't know whether the Soviet infantry is in this area. It can't be ruled out. Our nerves are tense. My submachine gun lies across my knees.

The silence around us is almost unbearable. The wind carries the sound of machine-gun fire from Nordenburg. A flare rises into the sky here and there.

We reach Waldeck after a good half-hour without incident. The place is empty. My driver accelerates without being prompted. He wants to get out of this village just as much as I do. The empty windows in the small number of houses look potentially hostile.

After we've left the last house behind us, we come across a forest. That explains where the name of the village has come from. The driver brings the car to a stop. He looks at me questioningly. I am once more faced with the question of whether or not to do something. Once again I have to make a decision that could determine not just my fate but also that of someone else. And that someone else has to accept my decision regardless of whether it is right or wrong. Who can definitively say in this situation what is right and what is wrong?

I take a deep breath. 'Onward!'

The Volkswagen struggles slowly through the snow. The edge of the forest lies to our right. If we stray even a little off the track, the branches will brush our vehicle. An open area of snow lies to our left. I start sweating under my cap.

Finally, the forest to our right retreats from the track. We roll slowly towards the western outskirts of Ellernbruch.

Something moves on the village road in front of us. It calls out: 'Halt! Who goes there?'

'Don't shoot!' I reply.

A platoon of 'Hermann Göring' grenadier troops has taken up a position of all-round defence, as is so often done when no one has any idea where front and rear are. I speak to the platoon leader, a sergeant, and he already knows about the Russians at Neusobrost.

I ask for directions to Plattau. The sergeant replies: 'Keep going straight and turn left at the next fork in the road. The road is being subjected to fire every now and then. No one can be seen there during daylight anyway. Ivan has reached the Bruchort–Plattau road.'

The sergeant accompanies us to the village exit and wishes us a safe journey.

The blanket of snow on the road is firm, which means that we make rapid progress and, after just two kilometres, can see the houses of Plattau in front of us. We are approaching the estate a short time later when a mortar attack commences.

My driver, who's also heard the howl of the mortar shells, steps hard on the accelerator. The command car shoots forward and soon screeches to a halt inside the estate. We manage to take cover just before the next salvo crashes into the roofs of the buildings.

I report to Captain Wolf and inform him of the new situation. He looks as if he is about to say something when I tell him of the extension of the defensive sector, but he just shakes his head instead and reaches for a cigarette.

25 January: The night is quiet. There are brief sounds of battle here and there, but no serious assault is launched by the Russians.

A heavy firefight is underway on the left wing, opposite Klein Pentlack, at 06.10. The telephone rings at that moment. A corporal is on the other end. 'Ivan was in our trench just now. We managed to repel him.' There is a short pause. 'No one's come back.'

Four wounded men arrive shortly after 0700 hours. Thank God they can still walk. After the medical officer has bandaged them, they are sent off to Dreimühl. It is still dark. They will be able to reach the dressing station.

Ivan has become active by 12.10. Our farmstead is under artillery fire. The wind whistles through the shattered windows. Russian infantry forces are advancing westwards through the open terrain between Plattau and Hochlindenberg. No one can stop them. Even to our south, in the vicinity of Bruchort, the noise of battle is getting louder. Ivan is simply letting us stay in our forest positions. He knows that we'll fall into his hands without a fight sooner or later.

The relationship between the strength of a unit and the task it is expected to carry out has become unmanageable. Approximately 80 fusiliers are being asked to hold a sector almost two kilometres in width, and that is without heavy weaponry.

The battalion commander takes action. He orders that the men at the northern end of the forest opposite Klein Pentlack withdraw to the Plattau estate with its front facing to the north-east.

By 13.30, the remaining elements of the battalion have conducted a fighting withdrawal to the farmstead.

Ivan is on our doorstep. I can clearly hear his shells exploding against the walls of the buildings.

The commander rushes outside. He gathers together the men who've taken cover nearby and, in close combat, hurls back the Russians who've occupied the houses on the other side of the road.

Ivan has suffered heavy casualties. Three fusiliers have also fallen in battle.

The captain returns. 'Go along the main line of resistance and try to determine what our strength is!'

I go outside. A Russian and two fusiliers lie dead at the north-west corner of the manor. The entire lower jaw of one of them has been ripped off by a piece of shrapnel. I have to look away.

My task doesn't take long. I am standing in front of the commander ten minutes later. 'Captain, the combat strength of the battalion is less than 50 men. We have almost expended our ammunition.'

Only 12 days ago our strength was more than 600 men.

The captain comes to a decision. 'See to it that any ammunition remaining with the fallen is gathered.'

The noise of battle flares up outside again. The commander goes to the window. A bullet strikes him in the shoulder at that moment. His arm is also wounded, and he begins to stagger. I just manage to grab him and, with the help of a messenger, lie him down on a sofa. His face is pale. Blood soaks his camouflage jacket.

I call for a medic. The commander's wound is bandaged a short time later.

Captain Wolf manages to speak. 'Knoblauch, take command of the battalion. I wish you and your men the best!'

I've always dreaded this moment. It isn't the task of leadership but rather the weight of responsibility that I can almost physically feel. It is a responsibility with two components: one towards my men and the other towards military duty.

Captain Wolf is removed from the danger zone on a trough-like sled pulled by two men who made use of the cover provided by the farmstead.

The noise of battle rises to a crescendo. Ivan enters the farmstead. I go to the door and down the wide flight of stairs that lead to the courtyard.

At the foot of the stairs, I see two Russians ten metres in front of me. They are just as surprised as I am. I react more quickly and see their distorted facial expressions as I raise and fire my submachine gun. They don't survive.

A squad of Russians has entered the south-east corner of the farmstead. They are shooting wildly. I dash up the stairs and reach the door at the last moment. The door panel behind me splinters as it is struck by bursts of submachine-gun fire.

Standing well back in the room, I look through one of the windows at what's going on in the courtyard below.

An MG 42 fires from the cover of a barn opposite me into the Russian squad. That deals with the situation very quickly.

I cautiously step outside into the courtyard. The Russian losses are enormous. Two of our men are dead.

I inspect our positions. All the men tell me the same thing: 'Our ammunition is running out!'

It is a desperate situation. I gaze to the west from the top of the manor staircase. I can see waves of Soviet infantry and armour through my binoculars. Two T-34s are burning in front of the positions of the 4. Regiment near Dreimühl. Ivan's spearhead is already three kilometres behind us. A tank column near Hochlindenberg is advancing westwards and encountering no resistance. To the south, the Russians have pushed beyond Ellernbruch and are rapidly advancing on Waldeck. My collar feels tight around my neck. The men around me look at me wordlessly and with concern. They know that their fate now depends on my decision. If I order that our position be held, they will remain without protest to continue the fight, and they will either die or fall into the hands of the Russians.

I come to a different decision and call for Second Lieutenant Schneider and Master Sergeant Staguhn. 'The battalion will break out to the west. Staguhn, you will assemble the remnants of the companies in the forest 2,000 metres behind us and then attempt to establish contact with German formations. Take care that no wounded are left behind. Don't forget that we have been subordinate to the

Grenadierregiment 45 since yesterday. I will remain here with Second Lieutenant Schneider and two fusiliers and cover your withdrawal.'

My order to withdraw is clearly a decision that has been made without the approval of the regiment. Perhaps I'll have to answer for this at a later stage. But I suppress my concerns. I don't have time for them with everything else that is happening right now.

Schneider, two fusiliers, and I set off diversionary fireworks with the remaining ammunition. Once on the left side of the courtyard and then on the right.

The remnants of the battalion are already 600 metres behind us. I look at my watch. It is 15.40. I hope that Ivan won't notice what is going on too quickly.

I can see from where I've taken cover that Ivan is launching another attack from the east. It looks like an entire battalion, and it's only 400 metres away.

There is no possibility of further diversionary action. I call out to Schneider and the fusiliers: 'Fall back!'

I see both fusiliers running across the courtyard. There is a burst of machine-gun fire. Both men fall to the ground. Dead! There is an awful taste in my mouth.

I rush to the west, making use of the cover provided by an elongated barn. I can see Schneider on the other side of the courtyard. Soviet anti-tank guns open fire. The shells explode against the wall of a house.

I've left the courtyard behind when infantry fire starts up to my right. It is only 100 metres away. The fire forces me to take cover behind a large heap of manure. It is difficult to breathe.

My repeated attempts to get out of this situation are unsuccessful. The heavy fire keeps me pinned down behind the manure.

Fear – tremendous fear – rises inside me. I have to make a decision. Immediately. No turning back.

Should I allow myself to be taken prisoner behind this heap of manure, only to be shot? Or should I tempt fate and take flight across the open terrain?

I put aside my map-mounting board and thrust the muzzle of my submachine gun into the soil. Then I leap forward with wild determination and dash away.

I'm struck by fire from the right. I keep running, my vision hazy. If I lose my nerve now, I'll be a dead man. I run as much as the soft soil and the melting snow allow.

A glance to my right and I almost freeze. A company of Russians have risen from a trench which runs parallel to my direction of flight. They are moving towards me and shooting away.

I keep running. But I am slowing down. My strength is diminishing. I fall to the ground.

I have no idea how long I lie unconscious in the muddy snow.

From somewhere far away I hear someone call: 'Get up!' Then there are bursts of fire from a submachine gun.

When I come to my senses, I see Second Lieutenant Schneider next to me. He is keeping the Russians at bay with his submachine gun.

The fear brings me back to my feet. I can taste blood in my mouth. I spit it out and cough violently. Then there is more blood in my mouth.

Schneider and I rush on. The Russians have come closer. I can clearly see their unshaven faces and their open coats and can hear their unnerving bellowing.

They are shooting from their hips. Bullets whistle past us. It is a miracle that we haven't been hit yet.

My strength is diminishing again. I can't go on. My knees buckle. I fall. So, this is the end, I think. But Schneider should try to save himself. 'Schneider, get out of here!' That's all I can manage. I lose consciousness again. When I come to, Schneider is changing the magazine of his submachine gun. I struggle to pull myself together. We slog through the wet, muddy snow.

My mouth is full of blood again. I spit it out. The bleeding gets worse with every coughing fit. My lung injury from 1943 is obviously causing trouble.

We still have 100 metres to go to the slope just before the forest where we want to hide. We are now moving behind the Soviet spearhead that is advancing on Dreimühl. The second wave of Russians have pursued us from the Plattau estate, and they are now breathing down our necks.

The Russians are shooting again. Even an anti-tank gun takes aim at us every now and then. I suddenly feel a stab of pain in the side of my chest under my left arm. Warm blood runs over my ribs and flows over my waistband. But I can still walk. Fear keeps me going.

We reach the forest. I slowly grasp the fact that we've escaped from Ivan. For now!

The Russians are probably full of vodka, otherwise we surely would have been hit.

'Without you, Schneider, I'd be a dead man!' I blurt out.

'I couldn't leave you high and dry!' responds Schneider.

I know at that moment what good comrades we are.

We feel our way through the forest to the west. We stop every now and then and listen. Where is Staguhn with the remnants of the battalion?

It has become dark. The forest seems a bit sinister. There are cracking sounds in the undergrowth here and there. I suggest to Schneider that we step out into the open space by the southern edge of the forest and proceed carefully to the south. There have to be German troops somewhere.

A few hundred metres from the edge of the forest, we take one step at a time towards the south.

Schneider takes my arm after a few minutes and points ahead without a word. A black speck can be seen in the distance on the wet snow. It might be a shed. Or a tank.

We approach slowly, our fingers on our triggers.

After 30 metres, I hear the safety catch of a carbine being flipped and someone shouting: 'Halt! Who goes there?'

'Don't shoot! We're German!'

We approach carefully and come across a German assault gun.

From the hatch, a second lieutenant calls out, 'Who are you? And where have you come from?'

'First Lieutenant Knoblauch, Fusilierbataillon 2 "Hermann Göring". This is Second Lieutenant Schneider. We've been under the command of the Grenadierregiment 45 since yesterday. We've just escaped from the Russians. We came from the forest over there.'

'Unbelievable. The forest is full of Russians. I've been ordered to keep an eye on the forest to ensure the security of the Nordenburg–Gerdauen road for our retreating formations. I'll be leaving in ten minutes. You can come with me. I'll take you to the regiment.'

When it is time to go, the driver starts the engine. I am given a spot in the assault gun, and Schneider sits atop the vehicle.

The assault gun rocks back and forth as it makes its way back to the main road. I crouch on my primitive seat and try to stop my head from hitting the steel plates. The cold wind rushes in through the slits in the vehicle and prevents me from sleeping despite my exhaustion. I no longer have any idea what is going on around me.

I am vaguely aware that the assault gun comes to a stop and that its engine is then switched off.

The assault gun lieutenant taps me on the shoulder. 'We're here. We're at the command post of the Grenadierregiment 45 in Wandlacken.'

I feel weak. Schneider helps me out of the steel monstrosity, and I wave to the assault gun lieutenant. 'Thank you!' I say.

Schneider and I enter the regimental command post. In the room, half lit by candlelight, are a number of officers and men. A map lies on the table.

A colonel rises from a chair. He is a tall man. He wears the Knight's Cross. This is without question the commander of the 45th.

I salute. 'First Lieutenant Knoblauch and Second Lieutenant Schneider of the Fusilierbataillon 2 "Hermann Göring". We covered the withdrawal of the battalion from the Plattau estate and have now lost contact with it. Colonel, I request …'

I trail off. My weakness has taken hold of me again, and I pass out. I have no idea how long I am unconscious for. When I come to, the colonel comes over to speak to me. 'Second Lieutenant Schneider has reported to me what happened. You will get the papers you need from your battalion doctor, who has also arrived here in Wandlacken, and you will then go to the nearest assembly point for the wounded. Second Lieutenant Schneider will assume command of the battalion. As far as I know, he is the last remaining officer of the fusiliers. Your men have found shelter in Linde. That is a good 1,000 metres north of here. I will let you go there.'

I go to see Dr Naumann. He treats me and hands me a wound tag. The injury to my torso is harmless. It is a four-centimetre wound under the left arm, almost as if it had been cut open with a scalpel. The lung haemorrhage is worse. 'No physical exertion,' orders the doctor. 'No running.' He must have known that this advice was unrealistic.

A car takes Schneider and me to Linde. The fusiliers have been given accommodation in separate houses. I can't speak with anyone. The men are dead tired and fast asleep.

Despite our frayed nerves, Schneider and I also try to get some sleep.

26 January: It is just after 0800 hours. I hear a car driving up outside. Someone calls for Second Lieutenant Schneider, who goes out to the village road and comes back a short time later. 'I need to go to Wandlacken to receive orders. The battalion is to attack eastwards from here at 0900 hours. We'll be led by a battle group commander whose command bunker is 600 metres north of Linde. Please get the men on their feet. I'll be quick!'

It isn't easy to wake the men. I get them to fall in. We proceed northwards along the road to the battle group headquarters. Sounds of battle can be heard in the Astrau Forest to our right.

The commander of the battle group, a captain, sits in a small concrete bunker. I go inside and inform him of the arrival of the fusilier battalion.

The captain appears to be nervous and irritable under the weight of his responsibility. Without any introduction, he gives the order for an attack to be launched on the western edge of the Astrau Forest, almost as if he expects it to be done on the spot.

I have some difficulty in getting him to understand that I no longer belong to the battalion and that Second Lieutenant Schneider will be there in a few minutes with the final orders of the regiment.

The conversation becomes somewhat heated. I decide to leave the bunker before it escalates. I meet Dr Naumann at the entrance and tell him what has happened. 'Doctor, do me a favour and make it clear to the commander in there that I can barely even walk ten metres!'

A wounded man is brought in on a stretcher at that moment. His face is pale green.

Dr Nauman addresses the stretcher-bearer: 'What's wrong with him?'

'Shot in the stomach, Doctor!'

Dr Naumann examines the wounded man. There is a small bullet hole below his navel. There is no blood. The doctor feels the abdominal wall and, to my surprise, pushes a pointed bullet out of the wound. It had been lying flat under the abdominal wall and hasn't caused any further injury.

The wounded man realises how lucky he's been. The colour returns to his face.

An assault gun rolls up on the road. Second Lieutenant Schneider is sitting on top of it. The vehicle comes to a halt and Schneider jumps down. 'We will attack immediately. The edge of the forest over there needs to be taken before Ivan is reinforced.'

We say goodbye to one another. I wish Gert Schneider all the best and then make my way to the assembly point for the wounded.

From the East Prussian Pocket to the Reich, January–March 1945

The wounded sit and lie in the rooms of a small house. Warm beverages are being handed out. Everyone is waiting to be transported away by ambulance.

We are still waiting at 1600 hours. I am feeling uneasy. If Ivan breaks through at Wandlacken, he'll take us prisoner here.

The noise of battle is carried over to us on the wind. I go to see the master sergeant who is in charge here. 'Do you still expect the wounded to be picked up by ambulances or other vehicles?'

He looks at me with concern. 'I no longer think it likely, First Lieutenant.'

That is enough for me. I ask for a dry slice of bread, leave the house and take the road to Gerdauen. I have no baggage. I haven't had any for a long time.

It is getting dark by 16.40. A small village lies ahead on the right-hand side of the road. I get closer and read the village sign: Prätlack.

I see a faint light behind a darkened window. I approach the house, knock and go inside. I see a couple with their daughter in the kitchen. The man is about 50 years old and the daughter probably 15. I can't estimate the age of the woman. They are sitting at a large table and staring into the flickering flame of a candle that has almost burned out. The man stands up as I enter and pushes a chair towards me.

These people are on the run. They know that the situation is hopeless and that a difficult decision confronts them. To break the awkward silence, I say, 'Will you spend the night here or go further west now?'

'We don't know yet,' replies the man in a rough East Prussian dialect. 'We don't know anything any more!' He stands up and paces back and forth, then comes to a stop and turns to me. 'I can tell you that I was the local group leader not far from here. The residents of our village left a week ago. I stayed here with my family. The local group leader can't simply make a run for it, certainly not with the first group that leaves. Now we're here and don't know what to do next. I remained firm in the belief that the Führer wouldn't abandon us.' Quietly, he adds, 'He's betrayed us.'

I don't know what to say. This man is old enough to be my father. He's lost not only his homeland but also his faith in everything. That loss of faith is the worst thing of all!

So that the conversation doesn't fizzle out, I ask for directions to Gerdauen and Schippenbeil.

The man reaches for his briefcase. As he takes out his map, a 7.65mm pistol falls onto the table.

We look at one another. The man gestures towards his pistol. 'You should also know that we won't fall into the hands of the Russians.' This is a statement I've often heard in recent months.

I am out of my depth in a situation like this. I can't help these people. I stand up slowly. I reach the door and glance back into deeply sad eyes. Without saying goodbye, I step outside. I shiver.

A truck stops at the side of the road. The driver, a non-commissioned officer, is happy to give me a lift.

We drive to Gerdauen via Altendorf. We are stopped on the outskirts of Gerdauen. It has become clear as we've approached that checks are being carried out by the military police. The truck driver shows his transport order and I my wound tag. We have no problems and are able to continue.

Gerdauen soon lies behind us. We are now on the road to Bartenstein. The driver stops the truck after another ten kilometres. 'This is my unit, First Lieutenant. I'm not going any further.'

I thank him and get out.

A long column of horsedrawn vehicles moves along the road to the south-west. The temperature has dropped. The moisture on the road has frozen so that it's as smooth as glass. I can only make slow progress under these conditions. I remain in the lee of one of the wagons to protect myself from the sharp wind. The draught horses have cloths tied to their hooves to reduce their risk of slipping. Other soldiers, alone or in pairs, are walking with me in the direction of Schippenbeil.

It is a depressing sight. Here are the apathetically traipsing soldiers of a disintegrating army and the column of horsedrawn vehicles with men who are just about to lose their Fatherland and who are heading for an uncertain future.

We pass through a small village. The old man on the wagon next to me says that it is Dietrichsdorf.

Half an hour later, I can feel my strength waning. My legs can't support me any more. I am on the verge of total exhaustion. There'll be no help if I collapse here. I can't keep up with the pace of the horses, so I come to a stop. The column moves on. Something flares up on the horizon behind me. Artillery fire.

Although it is dark, I am able to see a building a little way off to the right of the road. I walk slowly towards it. It is a barn.

I know that I have to stay here for a little while to regain some of my strength. I am starting to feel hungry.

I carefully open the door of the barn and go inside. To my great surprise, the interior is filled with soldiers. Many of them lie on the ground. It is difficult to move about without inadvertently disturbing someone.

I close the door behind me and remain a moment to listen. It isn't easy to see everything in the dark, but I know the barn is packed. The odour is overwhelming.

I crouch down and, after a quarter of an hour, I find a spot on the ground.

Although I am exhausted, I find it difficult to sleep at first. I keep thinking about the situation I am in. If I want to get out of the East Prussian pocket, I will need sufficient physical strength as well as the courage to take risks. Anyone who allows himself to be swept up by the events taking place will surely perish.

So exhausted am I that eventually I fall asleep.

27 January: I feel myself shivering. It is so cold that I've woken up. I look at the luminous dial of my watch. It is shortly after 0500 hours. I get up slowly, make my way carefully to the door, and step outside. It is still dark.

My legs feel stiff, but I get myself moving and go back to the road.

Flares are floating in the sky far behind me, and the noise of battle can be heard to the south. If the soldiers in the barn don't wake up soon, they'll most certainly be woken up by Ivan.

The road is empty. There is neither vehicle nor soul in sight. I walk slowly and eventually come across a truck parked on the side of the road just outside Schippenbeil. The driver gives me a lift.

We arrive in Bartenstein at 06.30. I get out in front of the local hospital. The place is overcrowded. I manage to get a spot on a mattress on the floor and, for the first time in several days, my first warm meal. It is barley broth. Then I lie down on my mattress and go straight to sleep.

I am woken by a state of unrest in the hospital. I go out to the hallway and ask what is going on. A medical sergeant tells me that the wounded who are able to walk are going to be sent that morning in an improvised hospital train in the direction of the lagoon.

'Why the hurry?' I ask.

'The Russians took Lötzen yesterday and are advancing on Rastenburg, and it's only two days' march from there to Bartenstein. I've also heard that Ivan is at Elbing. If that's so, we'll be cut off from the Reich!'

I know that that's true.

Those who are able to walk are going out in a long line to the station. Many of them have suffered wounds to the leg or foot. They are not really able to walk properly, but their understandable fear of the Russians has made them mobile.

There is a train with goods wagons at the station. We clamber into them. Old, musty straw has been laid out in the wagons.

I lie down straight away to rest. It is important to gather as much strength as possible now for the tremendous exertion that no doubt still lies ahead.

The train departs at 11.30. The temperature has risen. It's started to snow heavily. We make only slow progress. We can't know for certain why this is the case.

We go through Heilsberg and arrive in Landsberg, in East Prussia, at 2200 hours. The train comes to a stop.

I get out my flashlight and my small map of East Prussia. I realise that we've headed north rather than west. Has Wormditt already been taken by the Russians?

An hour has gone by before the train starts moving again. I am getting really hungry. And there is nothing to drink.

We stop on a stretch of track shortly before midnight. I try to get some sleep.

28 January: Hunger wakes me up. It is 0700 hours. We are still stationary on a stretch of track in the middle of a forest. It is snowing nonstop. I am freezing and miserable. The wind is carrying the sounds of battle to us.

A general staff major and an elderly captain are sitting on a crate on one side of the wagon. I gather from their conversation that the 4. Armee, which we belonged to, has been encircled. The Russians have reached Königsberg and have also got as far as the Vistula Lagoon west of Frauenburg. I haven't heard this news so clearly and precisely until now.

The wounded, who like me lie on the floor of the wagon, have overheard the conversation. Their reactions vary. Some appear apathetic in the deceptive security of the wagon. Others become anxious and start discussing how they might escape the impending imprisonment.

Only in the afternoon does our journey continue. We go through Zinten at 2000 hours.

The train comes to a halt again. I climb down from the wagon and grab a handful of snow to quench my thirst. The rising wind drives me back into the wagon. I lie down and try to sleep, but in vain. I think of my battalion and of Gert Schneider. I think of the fallen whose names aren't even known. Perhaps there isn't even anyone left alive who can notify their relatives.

29 January: We go through Heiligenbeil at walking pace and arrive at the platform in Braunsberg early in the morning. It has become broad daylight in the meantime.

It is announced that the train won't be unloaded today. That also means that there'll be nothing to eat or drink.

I get out and look around a little. There are no washing facilities.

I walk towards the edge of town at lunchtime. The enforced idleness is making me nervous.

In the hope of being able to wash myself, I ring the doorbell of an apartment. A middle-aged woman opens the door. I tell her what I want.

'Come inside,' she says.

In the hallway is a wardrobe with a mirror. I look in the mirror and see only a shadow of myself. The friendly woman opens the door to the bathroom, hands me soap and a towel, and tells me that there is also a razor that belonged to her son, who went missing six months ago in Normandy.

It occurs to me while shaving that it will only be a few days before a Russian will be shaving in front of this mirror. He'll certainly do more than shave in this apartment too. An unbearable thought.

I thank the woman as I am about to leave. She asks, 'Do you know what's happening in Hungary? My husband is there, and I haven't received any mail for a while.'

'I'm sorry, but I don't know what's going on in Hungary. We barely know what's happening here in East Prussia in any detail. All we know is that we're surrounded.'

I can see the concern in her face as I say goodbye to her.

30 January: We are still in the wagons at the platform in Braunsberg. The tracks haven't been cleared for any other trains. There are no more trains!

It is said that Korschen has fallen into the hands of the Russians. Their armoured spearheads have reached Heilsberg.

31 January: We are finally told to go to the hospital. We proceed in a long column into the centre of the town.

The situation in the hospital is utterly chaotic. It isn't anybody's fault. The circumstances are simply beyond the control of those in charge.

The wounded lie not only in beds but also on the floors in rooms and corridors. I am given a place to sit on the stairs.

Watery soup is served for lunch.

Catholic nuns and tireless medical staff do their best to provide relief to the wounded. The hospital staff will remain until Ivan is on their doorstep, although it is by no means certain that this admirable attitude will prevent the death of the wounded, given what usually happens to those who fall into the clutches of the Russians.

In the evening it is announced that those who are able to walk will march across the ice of the Vistula Lagoon to the Vistula spit. I can only hope that this will be done soon, while the ice is still strong.

1 February: I spend the night sitting on the hospital stairs. The rooms and corridors are filled with the nauseating smell of sweat, ether, urine and pus.

In order to get an overview of the situation, as far as that is possible, I go out to the outskirts of the town. Horsedrawn vehicles are arriving from Frauenburg. I speak to an old man and learn from him that they were on their way to Elbing but that they then came across the ring of encirclement shortly after Frauenburg. He is now looking for a hospital because his granddaughter is due to give birth today or tomorrow.

There is a constant rumbling in the air. The noise of battle is edging closer. I am feeling increasingly uneasy. The proximity of the Russians is ever more noticeable.

Medics are regularly walking past me. They are carrying those who've given up this life and who are therefore spared a great deal!

I go outside again at 1200 hours. I am still feeling uneasy.

To my surprise, I come across the horsedrawn vehicles that left Braunsberg and headed east yesterday and that are now moving again in the direction of Frauenburg. I can see the dismay in the faces of the people in the column. Ground-attack aircraft strafed the column in the vicinity of Grünau.

There is a sense of doom in the hospital. The medical staff are clearly nervous. Only the nuns demonstrate composure, even though they are the ones, given the mentality of the Red Army soldiers, who are facing a terrible fate.

2 February: It is morning. The windows are vibrating. The explosions of artillery shells are getting alarmingly closer.

I go to the office to enquire about the possibility of transport. A medical officer addresses me gruffly: 'What are you doing here?'

'I'm wounded, but able to walk. I'd like to know how I can get out of the East Prussian pocket.'

The medical officer looks at me. 'We are staying here, and so will you!'

I am furious. 'I don't think so, Doctor! You have a job to do here. I do not!'

I decide to go to another hospital. When I get there, a march group of wounded is being assembled. A senior medical officer is in charge.

I ask if I can join the group. The doctor nods. 'You've come just in time. You can lead this group. There are 40 wounded. Depart for Frauenburg when the sun has set. That will be at 1800 hours. We're hoping that the ice is still strong!'

We stay at a village inn and are given something hot to drink. It is a mystery to me who is in charge there.

There are 19 left in my group of wounded men. We go to bed early to get some sleep and regain our strength for resuming the march.

4 February: I gather my men at 0900 hours. 'Everyone, listen up! We're setting off now to finally get off the spit. Anyone faster than me needn't wait for me. It might be a matter of minutes whether or not we can avoid being taken by the Russians!'

We move off to the west in a long line. After half an hour, there are only a few men who are still with me. The march in wet shoes is disastrous.

An elderly couple are walking in front of me. The man could very well be a retired teacher. They pull a small handcart behind them with a suitcase. The woman carries a bulging bag and the man a backpack. They obviously have with them whatever they thought worth saving after a long life of hard work.

We are a short distance from Vogelsang when I hear a low-flying aircraft approaching from behind. 'Take cover!' I call out.

I can't believe my eyes. On the fuselage of a Ju 188 is the black cross and the characters 5 F + M, the identification of the 4.(F)/14. My comrades from the Münchhausen squadron are so close and yet unable to help.

The retired couple come into view again at 12.15. The two of them are walking slowly and tiredly ahead of me. They've left everything behind. The man only has his backpack. I can't imagine what might be going through their minds. Theirs is one fate among thousands!

Bodenwinkel lies before us at 1600 hours.

The bulk of the flow of refugees that have come from the spit pour into the open terrain to the west of the Vistula Lagoon. Countless numbers of people, both soldiers and refugees, come to a stop here. What is remarkable is that most of them now think they're safe.

I pause to rest for a few minutes. There are five men with me. Driven by some measure of anxiety, I force myself to get going again.

We reach Stutthof, and it isn't clear to me what to do next. I try to find out who is in charge there, but it is a hopeless undertaking.

Most of the people around me are in such a state of apathy that they are no longer capable of acting on their own initiative. Many of them don't even know where they are.

Artillery fire can be heard to the south. It is like a distant thunderstorm.

It has become dark. If something doesn't happen quickly, we'll soon fall into the hands of the Russians, powerless and exhausted. I look at my map and think how I can find a way to join up with units that are still engaged in combat. That will be far better than waiting idly to be taken prisoner by the Russians. And it won't be long before the Russians arrive.

In the evening, when it is almost 1900 hours, we are told to go to the railway station. I am awake at once and relieved that, despite the air of doom, action is still being taken.

I board the train of a narrow-gauge railway with many others at 19.20. We are all filled with hope.

We are still standing at the station in Stutthof at 2100 hours. The hope that had arisen is fading away. After two hours of agonising waiting, I am seriously considering leaving the train. But then it gets moving. It is now after 2300 hours.

The railway line runs almost parallel to Reichsstrasse 129. We make slow progress. The train keeps coming to a stop on the open track.

Ahead of us, to the south, there are flashes of light on the horizon. That is the front, and it is no longer too far away from us.

5 February: After a long journey, the train comes to a final stop. We are told to get off. On the station building I read: Tiegenhof. Utterly exhausted, the mass of wounded and stragglers stumble out of the wagons. Outside, instructions are being given in a sharp commanding tone: 'Fall in! Rank is irrelevant!'

I push myself forward to see what's going on. A detail of the Waffen-SS stands at the end of the platform, submachine guns at the ready. Anyone who doesn't have a wound tag is separated from the rest. I'm directed to a branch line platform with many others and told to board a narrow-gauge train that stands there.

The sorting process on the platform is finished at 0300 hours. The train starts moving slowly and leaves Tiegenhof station. We are to be taken to Dirschau.

I notice after a while that we are heading west towards the Vistula. Surely it would have been better to go via Neuteich? Has it already fallen into the hands of the Russians?

The train rolls forward at walking pace through the night. It is freezing cold in the compartments. Every night comes to an end eventually, so this one will too.

It has become light by 0800 hours. We stop at a small station. I go outside to get some exercise. A railwayman tells me that we are in Lichtenau, eight kilometres from Dirschau. The front is audibly close.

We reach Dirschau. 'Everybody out!' someone calls out from the platform. We walk, or rather traipse, in a long line through the town towards the local hospital. Many can't walk on their own any more. They support one another or use a branch as a crutch.

The procession of the wounded is a picture of misery. They are the broken remains of a shattered army that has reared up one more time to avert the looming demise of the Reich.

The inhabitants of the town – women and children and old men – stand at the side of the road. They look horrified at the sight of the utterly exhausted soldiers. They can sense the catastrophe that is approaching and know that it can't be avoided. They also know about the massacres of women and children that have been carried out by the Red Army in Nemmersdorf, Schulzenwalde and elsewhere. And Ivan is now only a few kilometres away from Dirschau.

The weak blocking forces will fight to the last. But they won't be able to prevent the catastrophe.

We finally reach the hospital! To my great surprise, I am given an actual bed. The bedsheets are no longer clean. They are covered in blood. But what does that matter?

I take off my shoes and lie down. I suddenly realise how tired I am, and I sink into a deep sleep.

I can feel someone shaking me. I slowly wake up. A medical corporal stands by my bed. I don't know him.

'Get up, First Lieutenant! An ambulance is waiting in the courtyard downstairs. There's still one spot available. We're going to the station. A train will be leaving to go further into the Reich in half an hour.'

'Thank you! But I'm so exhausted that I want to rest for now.'

The corporal persists: 'You should come with us, First Lieutenant. This will be the last train!'

'No, thank you. I don't want to!'

The corporal shrugs his shoulders and leaves.

I realise I am in a state where I can't properly assess the danger around me.

The corporal is by my bed again half an hour later. 'First Lieutenant, there's still a seat available in the cab of the ambulance. This is absolutely the last chance for you to get to the station!'

The primal instinct of self-preservation has reawakened within me. I pull myself together, put on my shoes and go with the corporal down to the courtyard.

The ambulance takes me, along with other wounded men, to the station. I thank the driver and get on the train, which departs after a short time. I am glad to be on my way.

We are only just outside Dirschau when the train stops. It seems to me that those responsible for traffic management have no idea which lines are clear. Only after dark does the journey continue, albeit very slowly.

6 February: We arrive in Karthaus shortly after midnight and come to a stop. It is bitterly cold in the train carriage.

Only in the afternoon do we get moving again. At this rate, Ivan will certainly catch up with us.

We travel west along the coast, all the while fearful that we might be overrun by the Russian armoured spearheads.

We come to a stop outside Hamburg on 10 February at 0800 hours. Heavy bombing raids have done severe damage to transport links.

Many a tragedy has unfolded on the train on the way from Karthaus to Hamburg. Some of the wounded, unable to receive medical attention, have died from sepsis. They simply perished, covered in blood and filth. The climax was the birth of a child. The 17-year-old mother was taken off the train with her newborn at a small station south of the Pomeranian coast.

We go through Hamburg that evening. The Hanseatic city lies in ruins.

11 February: The hours creep by slowly. We arrive in Oldenburg at 2300 hours and, to our surprise, are told to get off the train. We are accompanied on our journey to the hospital by the wail of the air-raid sirens.

There are untold numbers of wounded at the hospital. The medical personnel there can barely cope.

14 February: I hear news of what is going on for the first time in weeks. Allied bomber formations conducted major raids against Dresden yesterday. The number of casualties among the civilian population is said to be extremely high. Our front in the west is under great pressure. The situation looks bad!

I go on leave and travel to Hanover, arriving at my family home on the night of 18/19 February. I see my son for the first time. He was born on 10 February in Hahnenklee, in the Harz. I stand thoughtfully by his bassinet. He has no idea of the catastrophe into which he's been born. I feel helpless. What hopes had I attached to the birth of my son? High hopes! At least I have a son and heir if this war is yet to take me out of action in its final phase.

20 February: The Reich is subjected to constant aerial bombardment by Anglo-American aircraft. Fighting is taking place in the vicinity of Breslau. It seems that the city is encircled and that the people there are living between homes, workplaces and air-raid shelters.

21 February: I am trying to find a place in any hospital in Hanover so that I can be near my family. The chances are slim.

There is an air-raid warning at 20.55. The wailing of the sirens is ear-splitting. Our son is placed on a pillow and then put in a holdall. The rest of our baggage is ready in case we have to evacuate.

Along with everyone else who lives nearby, we hurry towards the bunker on Wallenstrasse. The concrete block provides a false sense of security. The people sit on benches, utterly exhausted, and hope that the night will pass without them being struck by a direct hit.

The air is stale. Little is said. I can feel people glancing in my direction every now and then. The question of how much longer we'll have to put up with this remains unspoken. Or it might be the question of why we soldiers couldn't put an end to this. But that also remains unspoken.

These tormenting questions don't matter. The worker diagonally opposite me and the many others in the dim light of the bunker will be producing more armaments for the war effort tomorrow morning.

22 February: We are given an all clear at 01.15. Tired and exhausted, we return to our apartment.

Despite the bombing that the transport links have been subjected to, the Reich postal service is still mostly functioning.

Only now do I learn that my fellow airman Peter Presber of the 1./Jagdgeschwader 3 (1st Squadron of the 3rd Fighter Wing) was shot down in his fighter in air combat with Allied bombers over Reich territory in April 1944. He was the son of the writer Rudolf Presber and was not only a sophisticated and sensitive human being but also a dependable comrade. He was different to those of us who were typical of the officer corps of the 4.(F)/14, but he would have very much liked to have been like us. He lacked the rough appearance of the typical German soldier. Now he's been killed in aerial combat. Perhaps he had the enemy in his crosshairs and reflected at that moment how he'd be taking one life or maybe even several. He paid for any such moment of reflection with his life. He'd borne no trace of hatred towards anyone.

3 March: Allied bombers have carried out a raid against Hanover, and it is only at 0200 hours that we leave the air-raid shelter. Even the outskirts of the city have been hit. Bombs have landed between Barthold-Knaust Strasse and Am-Haselbusch Strasse. Many houses have been severely damaged. Nearly all the windows in my family home are shattered. Roof tiles have slid down into the garden.

6 March: Air-raid siren at 20.45! We do everything as usual: son in the holdall, baggage in hand, and rush to the air-raid shelter.

People are queuing up in front of the bunker. Beams of light from the searchlight batteries sweep across the sky. Anti-aircraft guns have already opened fire in the distance. We need to hurry!

A fellow in the crowd of people behind me feels the need to make a joke about the rather unfunny situation: 'Lying in bed with my Annette. Arse barely warm, air-raid alarm!'

We've just sat down on the benches when a woman in the back corner of the room cries out 'My child! My child!'

She rushes past us and stumbles down the stairs. I follow her so that I can render assistance if it's needed.

She comes towards me at the exit with her baby in her arms. Tears run down her cheeks. What's happened? She'd been holding her two-month-old child in a pillow, but the child had slipped out in the crush at the entrance. Hundreds of people had stepped over the child, including the man who'd been in bed with his Annette. But the child hadn't been injured! With all the horrors I've seen in this war, I've often ask myself whether a merciful God exists. After this incident, I feel that the answer is yes.

7 March: The High Command of the Wehrmacht made the following announcement: 'Heavy fighting has flared up in the streets of Cologne. Since the commencement of the major offensive between the Roer and the Rhine on 23 February, more than 700 enemy tanks have been put out of action.'

The Wehrmacht communiqué on 8 March states that heavy combat is taking place with enemy tank forces whose spearheads have pushed as far as Remagen.

We spend night after night in the bunker. Stoically, the population put up with the tremendous stress caused by the terror from the air.

A call for volunteers was made over a loudspeaker in the bunker a few days ago. Help is needed in putting out fires in the area. I volunteer and go out into the night, heading towards wherever fires light up the sky.

Waves of British bombers fly over us in the direction of Berlin. Several single-family houses are burning on Pyrmonter Strasse. I go to one of them, climb the ladder, and reach a window on the first floor.

Hot embers waft towards me. Someone from below hands me a hose, and I immediately direct the jet of water at the burning roof beams.

It seems to me that I am just getting the fire under control when someone calls to me from below: 'Are you crazy? You can't flood my house! Get down from there!'

I climb down reluctantly. The house burns to the ground.

I don't manage to find a place in a Hanoverian hospital. I return to Oldenburg on 19 March.

The air-raid sirens are nonstop. Allied formations fly day and night and bomb the capital of the Reich and other major cities, almost without resistance.

The following is reported on the radio on 22 March: 'Near Oppenheim, the enemy's armoured spearheads were annihilated. In Worms, fierce fighting is taking place.'

It is reported on 24 March that our troops in Hungary have brought the Soviet advance to a halt to the north of Lake Balaton.

A travel permit created by Soviet propaganda. These were even directed at individual companies! However, every man knew what awaited him in Soviet captivity. There were barely any German deserters.

The orderly officer of the Fallschirm-Panzerfüsilierbataillon 2 'Hermann Göring', Second Lieutenant Küchel.

Second Lieutenant Gert Schneider, signal officer of the Fallschirm-Panzerfüsilierbataillon 2 'Hermann Göring', went missing in action in the withdrawal battles between Wandlacken and Heiligenbeil in February 1945.

View looking towards Girnen. The T-34 in the foreground was put out of action in October 1944.

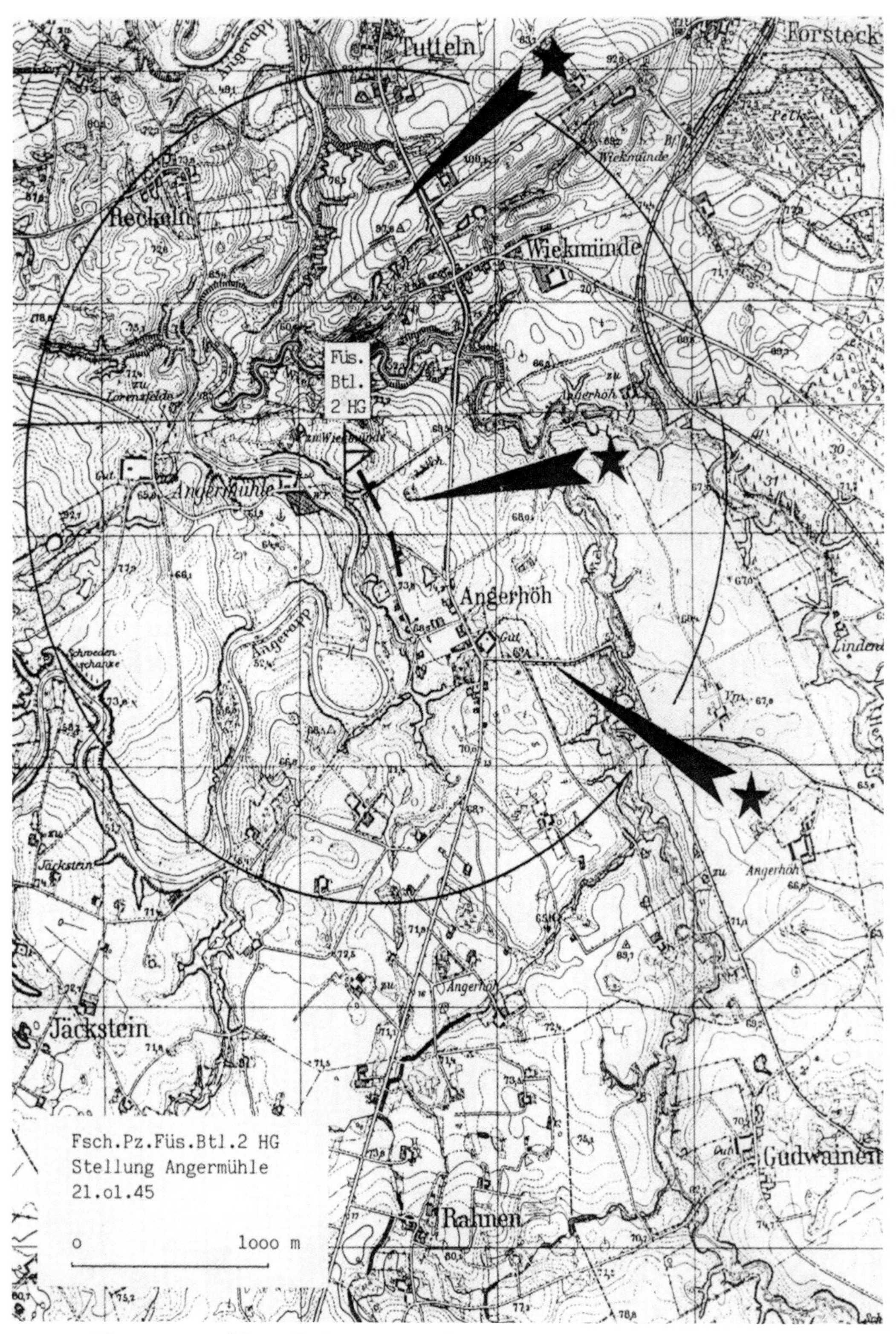

The position of the Fallschirm-Panzerfüsilierbataillon 2 'Hermann Göring' at
Angermühle on 21 January 1945.

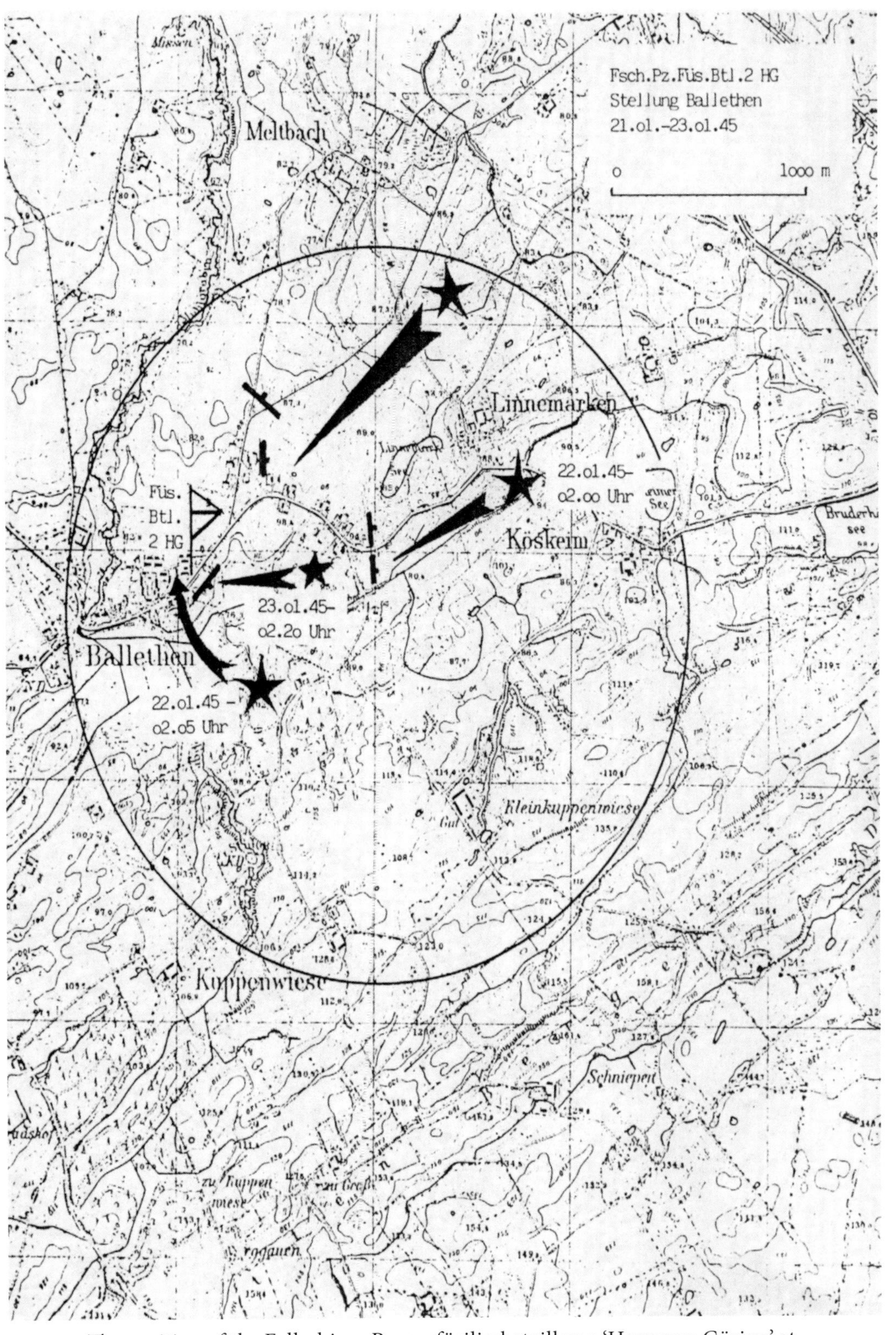

The position of the Fallschirm-Panzerfüsilierbataillon 2 'Hermann Göring' at Ballethen, 21–23 January 1945.

Red Army soldiers on a Stalin tank in a city somewhere in eastern Germany.

After the capture of the Seelow Heights by the Red Army in April 1945, vast masses of Soviet troops flooded towards Berlin.

Equipped only with small arms, these paratroopers attempt to stop the enemy. The German anti-tank rocket launchers were very useful.

Russian SU-85 assault guns roll through the streets with mounted infantry.

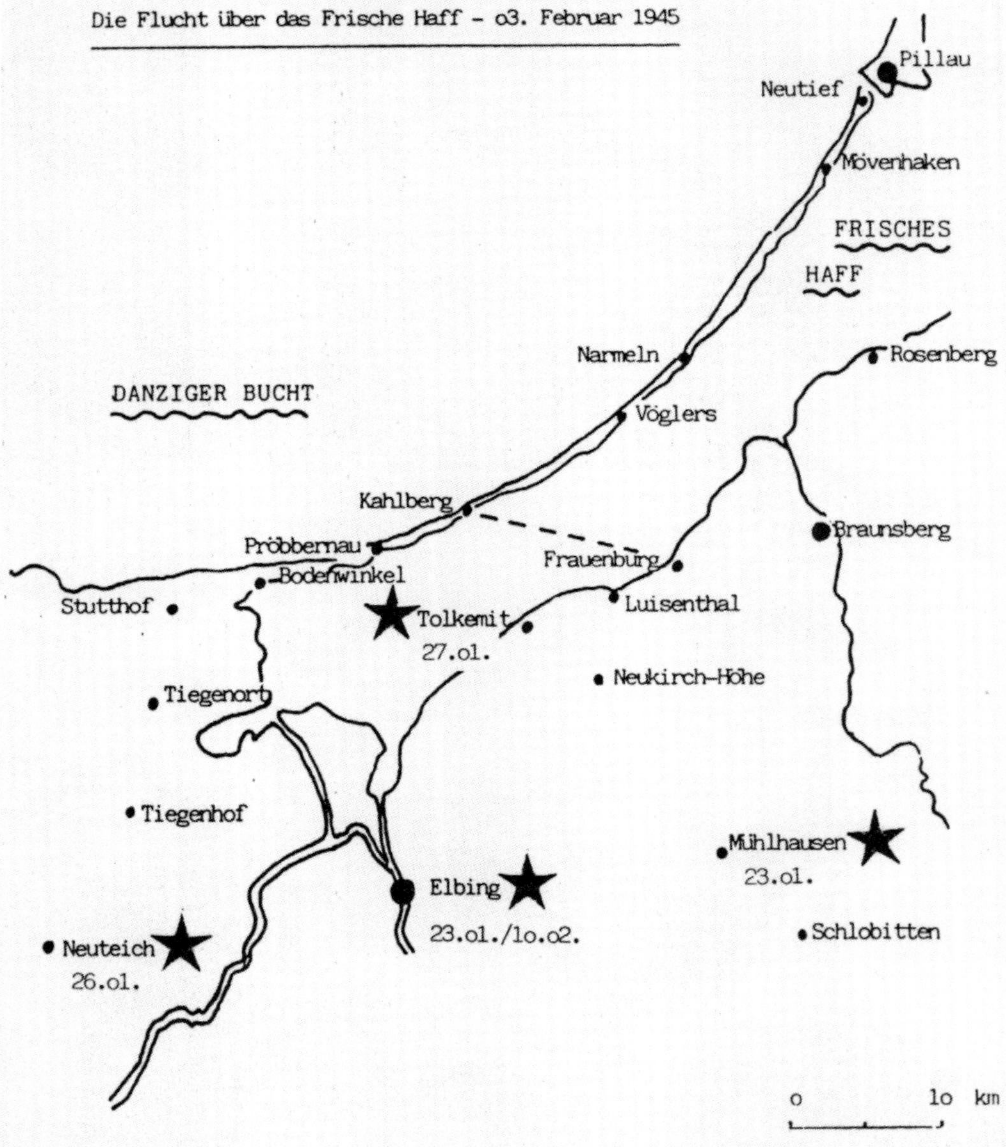

The escape across the Vistula Lagoon on 3 February 1945.

After fierce fighting, the Soviets captured the completely bombed-out city of Berlin in May 1945. Stalin tanks roll through the Brandenburg Gate.

The war is over, but not the suffering. These German soldiers are fleeing from the uncertain fate of captivity. Exhausted and hungry, they pause for a rest in the forest.

First page of the medal certificate dated 6 June 1945, written in a prisoner-of-war camp. Among the awards listed on this page, the Honour Goblet of the Luftwaffe has been lost, which is documented here as being awarded on 29 March 1943.

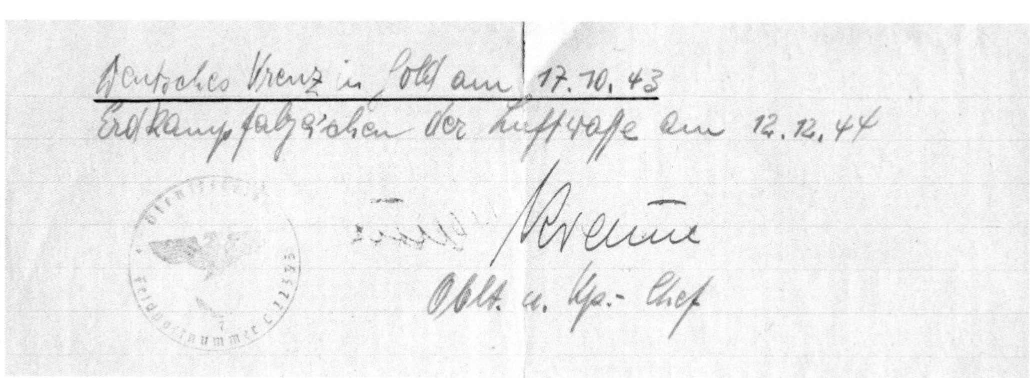

Second page of the medal certificate listing the German Cross in Gold and the Ground Assault Badge of the Luftwaffe, the latter being the last award received by Karl Knoblauch.

Luftwaffe Ground Assault Badge.

A reunion of squadron members in Bammertal, Heidelberg, in 1958. From left: Gerd von Szymonski, K. Heinze, Otto Lugscheider, H. Engelhardt and Karl Knoblauch. After the war, Otto Lugscheider contributed a great deal to the solidarity of the former comrades of the 4.(F)/14.

Wilhelm Schmalz and the former first general staff officer, von Baer,
at a 'Hermann Göring' gathering in 1981.

23. Jahrèstreffen der gepanzerten Kampftruppen
Kameradschaftsbund Fallschirmpanzerkorps
Munster 17. 11. 1985

A 'Hermann Göring' gathering at the Panzer Museum in Munster in 1985.

The popular former General Schmalz died in March 1983.

Karl Knoblauch and his wife Marion in autumn 2006.

On to the End, March–May 1945

25 March: British formations are advancing towards Oldenburg. The officers around me hold very different views about what to do in this extraordinary situation. Each man will have to decide for himself what to do.

As much as I want this war to come to an end, I can't quite accept the idea of being taken prisoner at this time. Not yet!

At my suggestion, the hospital administration issues me with travel orders. I will join the 'Hermann Göring' replacement troops in Veiten, north-west of Berlin.

26 March: I board a train shortly after midnight. The rail connection to the south is repeatedly broken. We only get as far as Cloppenburg.

It is afternoon by the time the journey continues. The drone of the Allied bombers can be heard above.

27 March: We go through Osnabrück and finally reach Löhne, north of Herford. This is the end of the line, as it has been destroyed by bombs from the air. We get out.

I decide to continue on foot along the railway embankment. Many others follow me on my march through the night. The herd instinct has taken over.

After almost three hours, we arrive in Bad Oeynhausen. No one there can tell us whether there'll be any trains today or tomorrow. No one seems to be in charge there any more.

I return to the railway embankment and march on. The group that has been following me has become smaller.

We come across a goods train beyond Vlotho. We get on board and arrive in Hameln in the morning. I can't go any further at that moment. I am physically exhausted and go to the local Wehrmacht barracks to get some sleep.

28 March: The situation at the front is unclear. There are no trains going to Hanover. My plan to head towards Berlin has to be put on hold for the time being.

I catch the train to Pyrmont in the morning. I am feeling anxious. It is no longer possible to assess the military or even the political situation. The Wehrmacht communiqué is confusing. The Americans are apparently in Darmstadt.

29 March: The news from the front is irritatingly confusing. The Wehrmacht communiqué states: 'North of the Danube, our troops are putting up resistance to the enemy to the west of Gran along the Nitra. In the north-western foothills of the High Tatras, advancing enemy forces were interdicted in a counter-attack. The brave defenders of Küstrin are engaged in heavy and self-sacrificing house-to-house fighting in the historic centre of the town. In Kurland, strong enemy attacks were repelled east of Libau, north-east of Frauenburg, and north-west of Doblen. On the Lower Rhine, the British and Americans only managed to expand their bridgehead at Bocholt, Borken and Dorsten and to push into Hamborn after six days of suffering bloody casualties and after the costly deployment of two airborne divisions. Enemy mobile formations advanced on narrow sectors through Wetzlar into the area of Giessen and Marburg and from a point of penetration at Hanau into the area of Grünberg in Hesse.'

30 March: Fighting is still taking place in East Prussia. What the empty words issued by the High Command of the Wehrmacht really mean can only be appreciated by those with experience of the conditions at the front: 'In the vicinity of the Gulf of Danzig, fierce fighting continued in Westerplatte and in the lowlands of the Vistula. After bitter urban combat and the utter destruction of the port facilities, Gotenhafen and Danzig fell into the hands of the enemy. Troops from all arms of the military, including supply troops and headquarters staff, fought in the front line. It is thanks to this determined fighting spirit that the front of the army has not been broken through at any point and that the enemy has had to struggle for every metre of ground in East Prussian territory through the heaviest losses in men and materiel. Due to the tough resistance put up by the 4. Armee in the period from 12 January until 28 March, the Bolsheviks have lost 2,557 tanks, 2,734 guns of all types, 307 mortars, 82 aircraft and 1,172 machine guns. Several thousand prisoners have also been taken.'

2 April: The explosions of artillery shells can be heard in Pyrmont. I have a decision to make. Pyrmont is a hospital town. A quiet departure would be possible there. But it isn't so simple. One's 'membership' can't be cancelled like in a sports club. Imprisonment? Not today!

I leave Pyrmont on foot on 5 April. There are no trains. The Americans have reached a point between Münster and Detmold.

Adventurous soldiers are walking along the road to Hameln. Some of them are pushing their baggage in prams. I don't have to worry about that. I no longer have any baggage.

The noise of battle can be heard from Lügde. Rumours are flying around. It is said that the Americans are already in Hameln. To avoid running into our brothers from across the sea, I leave the main road before the small town of Welsede and take a narrow lane that winds its way up to the heights west of the Weser. Stragglers from various units accompany me in the attempt to escape from the Americans. After two hours, we reach the Weser at Grohnde.

American fighter-bombers are flying over the road that leads from Hameln to Holzminden. I take cover in a passage that leads to the bank of the Weser. The ferry that used to connect Grohnde with the east bank has been sunk, and the ferry cable has been cut. I search for another way to cross the river and find a rickety boat.

I try with some effort to push the boat into the current when a harsh voice behind me calls out: 'The boat stays here!'

I turn around. An old man stands there and is gesturing threateningly. 'The boat belongs to me. You will not row across the river with it. The war is over. The Americans are almost here!'

The dull roar of tank engines reaches my ears.

I keep trying to set the boat afloat. The old man comes towards me with a wooden slat in his hands. Things are getting critical.

To shoot a man who wants to protect his own property is unthinkable. However, I absolutely want to determine for myself the time when I will be taken prisoner. And I have firmly decided that that time has not yet come.

I don't want to hurt the old man, so I have to bluff. 'Now look here! If you want to keep your boat, then row me across the river. You can do as you please after that, but you can't stop me. I'll use my weapon if I must!'

The old man gets in without a word. I breathe a sigh of relief.

With powerful strokes that I wouldn't have thought him capable of, the old man rows us towards the east bank of the Weser.

I look back towards Grohnde and the path that leads to the ferry berth. If the Americans arrive, that is where they'll be. And then there they are! A Sherman tank has appeared. It moves slowly towards the bank. The turret rotates, and the gun swings in our direction. I can see right into the barrel.

We are two metres from the safety of the bank. The old man pulls on the oars one more time. I jump out.

I splash through the water and dash for the nearest cover. The old man makes it to safety as well.

I carefully raise my head. The American tank hasn't fired. It could have blown us out of the water.

The turret hatch of the Sherman opens. The tank commander emerges to his waist, grabbing a pair of binoculars and looking over to us.

Unbelievable, I think. He wouldn't have been able to do that in East Prussia. There's no way he would have survived!

I take a few long strides, reach the road connecting Hameln and Holzminden, and roll into the roadside ditch. Low-flying American fighter-bombers dart by overhead, shooting at anything that moves on the road.

After 20 minutes, by which time the Sherman has moved away, I get up and go with some soldiers who've gathered here across the open fields to Börry.

Some women approach us on the outskirts of the village. They are in an agitated state. 'Move on quickly! We don't want any soldiers in our village. The Americans will be here soon. If shots are fired here, our children will be put in danger and our homes will be destroyed. And all at the last moment! We don't want to see any more German soldiers!'

I completely understand why these women feel the way they do, although it is painful to realise that soldiers are only welcome when they are victorious. That is the case for soldiers of all nations!

My heart sinks when I notice white cloths hanging from the windows. It is the first time I've seen such a thing on the German side in this war. I can't help but say: 'The cloths you have hanging there are so beautifully white that the Americans will most certainly respect them. Perhaps you might even be able to convince the GIs that there were never swastika flags in their place before!'

The women turn away in embarrassment. The soldiers around me grin.

Accompanied by a few stragglers, I go through Bessinghausen and reach the south-western slopes of the Ith at 1700 hours. Vehicles belonging to a panzer grenadier division, or at least those that are left after the fighting in western Germany, stand camouflaged under trees. A captain with whom I strike up a conversation tells me that the division will be withdrawing further into the Harz via Hildesheim once it gets dark. He is prepared to take me with him to Hildesheim.

Heavy rain has started in the meantime. We wait for the cover of darkness. No vehicle will be able to move on the road in daylight without immediately becoming prey to low-flying Allied aircraft.

The column gets moving at 18.45. The road winds its way up to the crest of the Ith. I am sitting in an open-top command car and get soaking wet.

We come to a halt. A motorised reconnaissance section is checking out the situation at the road junction in Hemmendorf, for this afternoon American columns have already been observed on the road from Alfeld to Coppenbrügge.

A grenadier company sets off at 2100 hours to secure the road junction.

Our column starts moving quickly at 2200 hours and reaches the outskirts of Elze 30 minutes later. It is pitch-black. Progress is slow after that. We go through Burgstemmen, Heyersum and Himmelsthür.

I jump off when we get to the northern outskirts of Hildesheim. Although it is dark, I can see that the city has been destroyed by bombing from the air. Rubble. Nothing but rubble. Remnants of walls lie on the road. The smell of burning permeates the air. It is 23.20 when I set off on foot on the road to Hanover.

6 April: I arrive in Gross Förste at 0100 hours. I see the faint glow of light behind the darkened window of a village inn. I go inside.

There are a number of Volkssturm men sitting at the bar. A party man asks me what I want. I tell him that I am simply looking for somewhere to sleep.

There are mattresses on the floor on one side of the room. I lie down and fall asleep from exhaustion.

By 0600 hours, I am feeling restless and get up. The Volkssturm men offer me a warm drink and a piece of bread. I am on the road again shortly afterwards.

In normal times, tram route 11 runs between Hanover and Hildesheim, but it isn't running any more. The overhead line is broken and has fallen onto the road in various places.

I walk briskly to Rethen via Sarstedt, Heisede and Gleidingen. I'm glad to see that there is a tram in Rethen ready to make its way to Hanover. All I have to do is hop on board.

I go through Wülfel and Döhren, get off in Waldheim, and walk along to the southern shore of Lake Masch.

The lake, which is so beautiful in peacetime, has been covered with floating green mats as camouflage. Artificial trees and bushes stand on top of them. This camouflage has hardly been any good. The industrial centres and residential areas of Hanover have been systematically bombed. Whole sections of the city lie in ruins. The casualties among the civilian population have been heavy.

An old man comes alongside me as I walk along the shore. 'Good morning, First Lieutenant!' he says with a hint of irony in his voice. He is on his way to Hanomag, the place where he works.

'Why aren't you taking the tram?' I ask.

'The transport connections in the city are destroyed, and the tyres on my bike are ruined!'

I try to think of something else to say. 'Why don't you stay at home?'

His response is quite remarkable: 'Believe me, I'm not one of those Nazi activists who are on the run! The war is lost, but I will go to work so long as our soldiers don't give up!'

I am taken aback. We walk side by side in silence. Our paths diverge at Ricklinger Stadtweg. The old man continues in the direction of Hanomag while I go home.

7 April: The Wehrmacht communiqué is ever more confusing. I want to get a clear idea of the situation and decide that I'll visit the Wehrmacht garrison headquarters in the city. I ride my bike to the city centre. I tell my family that I'd be back in an hour at the latest.

I ride past Schwarzer Bär to Waterlooplatz. The residential and business district between the Linden area and the railway station have been reduced to rubble. It is immediately noticeable that there are only a few people on the streets.

I turn right at the station forecourt into Joachimstrasse. A garrison headquarters office is on the right-hand side of the road. I go inside.

I come across a corporal on the first floor. 'Is there an officer around here?'

'There's no one here any more. The Wehrmacht offices have been moved into the Harz. We are the last ones here and are leaving this afternoon.'

Noise can be heard from the street below. Someone comes running up the stairs. 'The Americans are on Hildesheimer Strasse!'

I can feel myself growing pale. I slowly descend the stairs and organise my thoughts one step at a time. My will once more feels the urge to resist the inevitable. I don't want to be taken prisoner. Not yet!

My decision is made. I grab my bike and ride off in the direction of Aegidientorplatz.

I can hear low-flying aircraft as I enter Marienstrasse. I take cover behind the remnant of a wall, and not a moment too soon. Two fighter-bombers appear from behind the opera house and fly along Georgstrasse at the level of the burned-out roof trusses, shooting at anything that moves.

Once they've gone, I push my bike over to Hildesheimer Strasse. There is no sign of the Americans. Either someone has made a report in a panic, or the enemy sent armoured reconnaissance into Hanover and then pulled it out again.

As crazy as it seems, it is clear to me that I now had to ride to Berlin. What bothers me is that I won't be able to let my family know.

Even though I know that Ulli would do everything humanly possible for our son, I am still very worried. But I can't do anything for my family in this difficult situation. If I stay at home, the Americans will simply take me prisoner!

I ride through Kleefeld and Kirchrode and come across the Hindenburg Lock in Anderten. The streets are empty.

I go through Höver at 1100 hours. The village is deserted. There is no one to be seen. I am getting a bad feeling about this.

I slowly approach Bilm. The road curves slightly to the left through the town. Suddenly I see a group of people only 30 metres away. They aren't German!

I dismount and assess the situation. In front of me are about 20 foreign workers, probably Poles.

Some more appear behind me. I can feel the sweat on my forehead. I can't go back.

The expressions worn by these men do not bode well. In their hands are clubs and wooden planks.

They don't have any guns, I realise, otherwise they wouldn't be carrying clubs. I draw my pistol and slowly approach the group ahead of me.

I get to within 10 metres. The wretches don't move. They look at me with expressions full of hatred. Any false move by me will result in catastrophe. If they try to attack me, I'll shoot. No doubt about that.

I stop and say calmly but firmly: 'Clear the road!' I emphasise my words with a gesture of my right hand, in which I'm holding the P38.

The group start to move back hesitantly, one by one, but not far enough. If I get caught in the middle, I'll be done for.

With an unmistakable wave of my pistol, I indicate to those on the right-hand side of the street to move over to the left.

Luck is on my side, and I don't lost my nerve. The wretches move over to the left.

I quickly push my bike through the part of the street that they've cleared.

Keeping an eye on them, I mount the bike and pedal hard to gain some distance.

I get through. I've made it. The men behind me roar like animals, over and over: 'German pig! German pig!'

Well, the 'German pig' rides away on his bicycle. He isn't slaughtered.

I struggle further along the poorly paved country roads. I go through Sehnde, Rethmar and Mehrum. I frequently glance up at the sky. I have to keep an eye on it. I reach the Reichsstrasse near Hämeler Forest and pause to rest under a bridge. I lie in the grass and look up at the sky. Fighter aircraft are circling over Peine. They are American, of course, for there are obviously no German ones left.

I get up after 20 minutes have passed. I can't stay here. I push my bike onto the highway. It feels strange that there is not a vehicle in sight. I mount my bike and pedal to the east. I have the entire width of the road to myself.

The bicycle I am riding was a gift from my father in 1936. It served me well until my last day of school. This will probably be the last time I'll ride it.

My somewhat wistful thoughts are suddenly interrupted. I can hear the gradually approaching sound of a low-flying fighter-bomber from behind and can see the circling manoeuvre of a fighter in front. I estimate the distance to the nearest cover is approximately 50 metres. It is the protective overpass to the south-east of Sievershausen.

I only just make it. As I throw myself into cover, a full burst of fire from the fighter's onboard cannon hails down onto the concrete surface of the highway. Stone fragments and ricochet shots fly everywhere.

The fighter pulls up. I start pedalling, my focus on the next overpass.

Again I take cover just in time. Again the hail of fire strike the road.

I decide to wait. The fighter disappears beyond the horizon.

I go through Peine without incident. Meerdorf lies on the left a few kilometres further on. I performed my fatigue duty there in the summer of 1938. The barracks are still standing there.

I leave the highway once I reach Wendeburg and ride towards Gifhorn via Meine. I need to find a railway line. I am fed up with pedalling, and it is still a long way to Berlin.

I am at Isenbüttel-Gifhorn station by 18.10. Luck is again on my side. A passenger train will be departing for Berlin at 1900 hours. No one can say for sure how far it will go.

I put my bike in the baggage wagon, and the train departs. It has become dark in the meantime.

Some old women board the train in Oebisfelde. They are carrying heavy baskets.

We reach Gardelegen at 21.50, and that is where the train will remain for the time being. No one knows if or when the train will continue its journey.

I try to get some sleep. The monotonous drone of enemy bomber formations can be heard above us as they fly towards Berlin. These endless waves of bombers encounter no German resistance whatsoever.

8 April: The train finally gets moving again. I glance at my watch. It is 03.40. We go through the northern part of the Colbitz-Letzlinger Heide. Large pine forests flank the railway line on either side.

We reach Stendal via Jävenitz, Uchtspringe, Vinzelberg and Möringen. It is dawn by then, and we are asked to get off the train. I fetch my bike and look around the station. Nothing is happening. Has the war already come to an end without us knowing?

I can't stick around here. I think it best to continue so that I can visit my grandparents in Grosswudicke. That will be another 25 kilometres along the railway line. I decide to take the narrow trail that runs alongside the tracks.

The ride along the railway embankment is more difficult than I imagined. I have to dismount frequently to lift the bike over points and signalling controls.

The Elbe lowlands to the north of Hämerten lie in front of me at 07.10, concealed by the morning mist. I am less than a kilometre away from the railway bridge which spans not only the river but also the lowlands.

I encounter a pioneer unit in the vicinity of the bridge. A captain approaches me. 'Where are you going, young man? This bridge is a restricted area!'

He realises as I get closer that this 'young man' is an officer. I inform him of my name and rank and add that I am on my way to join the replacement troops in Berlin.

The pioneer looks at me in disbelief. He obviously thinks me to be not quite normal. 'You want to go to Berlin? Do you think you'll be needed there at this stage?'

'No one is waiting for me in Berlin, Captain, but I'm not going there of my own free will. I have travel orders that state that I am to go to the capital of the Reich. You'll no doubt understand that I'm reluctant to hide here in the bushes and wait for the war to come to an end. Such a decision could end with me hanging from a lamppost with a noose around my neck. I've done the right thing so far and will continue to do so until the last moment. I envy anyone who can stay with his own unit in these extraordinary times and who doesn't have to travel cross-country on his own like I do!'

The captain stops me with a wave of his hand. 'You're right, of course. But where's your former unit?'

'The battalion I belonged to was destroyed in January and February between Nordenburg and the Vistula Lagoon. I was wounded at the time, and it is thanks to that that I'm still alive today!'

The captain nods thoughtfully and shakes my hand. 'I wish you all the best. Have a safe journey to Berlin and, more importantly, back home afterwards.'

I salute with my arm outstretched in accordance with the orders that were issued in the wake of 20 July 1944. To my surprise, the pioneer tips his cap to me. He notices my state of surprise and smiles.

I ride to the bridge and then have to get off and carry my bike. Double sentry posts have been placed at intervals of 50 metres in between the iron arches of the bridge structure.

The large boxes of explosives that have been placed on the bridge and prepared for detonation encourage me to make haste. If an American aircraft opens fire on the bridge with its onboard weaponry, the bridge and all the pioneers on it will be blown sky high.

I quicken my pace. To my right, in the early-morning haze, I can see chimneys of the industrial facilities of Tangermünde.

The bridge lies behind me at last. After a few kilometres, I cross the road that connects Genthin and Havelberg. To the south, not far from where I am, lies Schönhausen. That is where Bismarck, the Iron Chancellor, lived. It was less than 100 years ago. But what a different place the world is now!

Beyond the lowlands of the Elbe, the railway line leads through almost impenetrable pine forests that extend from the Havel near Rathenow to the Elbe south of Sandau.

I come across a railway block station in the middle of the forest. I am thirsty and hope that I'll be able to get something to drink there. I lean my bike against a wooden fence and have a look around.

An old railwayman steps out the door. I estimate him to be well over 60 years old. He approaches me warily. 'What do you want here?'

'Do you have anything to drink?' I ask, then add: 'Are you always so unfriendly?'

The old man, in his shabby railway uniform, frowns. 'You have no idea what kind of rabble has been turning up here in the last few days. I have to be cautious!'

'And you think you'd stand a chance against such people?'

The man takes a step back and shows me a heavy double-action revolver. This surprises me. I've underestimated this person.

'Where did you get a cannon like that? Is it part of your equipment?'

'No, I got this thing from my father. He fought in the Franco-Prussian War. I never would have thought that I'd need to take the revolver out of the chest again!'

The ice is broken. I get a cup of water. Water rarely tasted so good as it does then.

I resume my journey a short time later. The old man waves goodbye.

I arrive in Grosswudicke shortly before 1000 hours. My grandparents are most surprised. I can see how much of a toll recent events have taken on my grandfather. He doesn't say anything about it.

My grandmother makes me something to eat. I go to sleep after that. I am utterly exhausted!

9 April: Fighting is still taking place in East Prussia. The Wehrmacht communiqué refers to heavy combat in Königsberg. A train is scheduled to arrive from Berlin the next day and then return shortly afterwards. My grandparents' house lies in the immediate vicinity of the small railway station. I'll keep an eye on developments.

On 11 April, the Wehrmacht communiqué announces the loss of Hanover. I can quietly tell myself that the war is finally over for my relatives. The situation there can hardly be worse than it has been in the previous few weeks.

12 April: The wind carries the noise of exploding shells from the west. The Americans are drawing closer to the west bank of the Elbe.

13 April: I walk through the village one last time in the afternoon as a kind of farewell. The locals have retreated to their homes and are waiting for fate to take its course. The streets are empty.

On the northern outskirts of the village, where the Gontard estate meets the road to Schollene, I come across an SS grenadier platoon. The young SS second lieutenant who is in command of the platoon tells me that Grosswudicke is to be defended. He says this so casually, as if he's talking about building a garden fence.

When I ask him about the situation, he responds: 'No situation is so bad that it couldn't get worse! We hardly know where the front is. Maybe this is where the final battle will be. Who knows? We'll keep fighting for as long as we have orders or until Ivan disarms us!'

His boyish face suddenly looks a lot older than I first thought. But he can hardly be more than 20 years old.

Deep in thought, I return to my grandparents' house.

It is a mostly quiet night. Only in the distance is machine-gun fire to be heard.

14 April: I get up early. I say goodbye to my grandparents and walk the short distance to the railway station, which is in fact nothing more than a halt point on the line between Hanover and Berlin.

A train does actually arrive this time. I get on board. I am the only passenger. It is obvious that no one but me has any intention of travelling to Berlin under the prevailing circumstances.

We cross the Havel at Rathenow. I often bathed there near the railway bridge when I was a schoolboy. But that's a long time ago. The landscape that is otherwise so familiar to me looks quite strange.

The train goes through Nennhausen and stops in Buschow. It was in Buschow and in the surrounding area that the estates of the old noble House of Knoblauch lay. My grandfather once spoke of it. But who cares about that now?

The train starts moving again. It does so slowly. It is as if the train were heading towards Berlin only with the utmost reluctance.

We go through Wustermark and Dallgow-Döberitz. It is between there and Gross Glienicke that Krampnitz lies, the military training school that I attended in September 1939. No one then could have thought that the war would last so long, let alone that it would be lost.

I get off the train in Charlottenburg. I look around and see ruins and rubble and can feel the sense of doom. Surprisingly, the city railway is still (or again) in operation. I travel to Reinickendorf to report to the Hermann Göring Barracks.

An American bomber formation appears overhead at 14.10. The aircraft are four-engined heavy bombers. They are known as Flying Fortresses due to their tremendous firepower.

A high-pitched noise clashes with the monotonous drone of the bomber engines. A single German fighter is to be seen in the cloudless sky, and it is diving towards the formation of approximately 40 bombers.

'He's crazy!' remarks a non-commissioned officer who is next to me. Perhaps he's right. But aren't we all crazy, especially those of us who haven't given up in the hopeless situation of the last few months? Who are we to judge what is crazy?

Above us is the staccato sound of the fighter's onboard cannon. In my estimation, the air battle is taking place at an altitude of between 6,000 and 7,000 metres. The German fighter flies in from below, commences a vertical climb, and opens fire. It shoots through the American armada and is then above it.

The German machine is remarkably fast. It circles around and dives down. Its onboard weaponry hammers away. One of the bombers begins to smoke and veers to the side.

I am mesmerised. I can clearly see that the German fighter has two engines. It is presumably a Messerschmitt Me 262. This is the miracle jet fighter that has been talked about so much.

The fighter makes another approach. The bombers open fire on it. The fighter fires back. A second bomber starts to smoke, and it soon falls from the sky in flames.

Yet another approach by the fighter results in a third bomber bursting into flames.

The fighter disappears beyond the horizon, and the bomber formation continues its flight to the west.

What I've just seen is unbelievable. The superiority of this fighter is incredible. I wonder why it has only now been put into service. Why so late? It is way too late!

15 April: No one at the Hermann Göring Barracks in Reinickendorf quite knows what to do with me. I am sent to Hohenschöpping, to the south of Veiten and in the north-western part of Berlin.

16 April: The Russians commence their assault on Berlin from across the Neisse and from the Oder bridgeheads.

The Americans crossed the Elbe in several locations yesterday. On the radio was the following announcement: 'To the south-east of Magdeburg, grenadier troops hurled the Americans who had advanced across the Elbe back to their jumping-off positions and took a large number of prisoners. Further to the south, counter-attacks are underway against other local bridgeheads.'

I receive orders to report to the headquarters of Fallschirm-Panzerkorps 'Hermann Göring'. It is located in Seftenberg, a place between Dresden and Cottbus.

In the evening, I board a train to take me to the corps headquarters.

17 April: I arrive in Seftenberg and have to ask for directions. No one is able to give a precise assessment of the situation, but it is clear to everyone that we are on the verge of collapse. This impression is dramatically amplified by the approaching artillery fire.

18 April: I report to the corps headquarters and am informed that the corps will not employ the 'physically disabled'. I am instead given orders to go to Veiten, Berlin, immediately.

It remains to be seen whether this decision will end up being good or bad for me. Who will get to Berlin first: me or Ivan?

I ride on a truck to Finsterwalde, and I am told at the station that there might be a train to Berlin at 2000 hours.

Outside, on the other side of the street, I can see women and children as well as some old men. As I get closer, I can hear them talking about the chances that might still exist of bringing the Red Army to a standstill.

I am surprised by the repeatedly expressed opinion that the 'Hermann Göring' units stationed in Hoyerswerda and Bautzen will be able to do it. Unbelievable! I turn away in embarrassment.

There is indeed a train that departs for Berlin at 2000 hours. The compartments are overcrowded with civilians as well as with soldiers from all branches of the military.

We get to within a short distance of Königswusterhausen by midnight and make no further progress after that. The tracks have been damaged by bombs.

19 April: The train reaches Eichwalde at 04.30. We are told to get off. I can see the searchlight beams over Berlin from the batteries stationed there.

I find a spot to sleep underneath an arbour a short distance from the railway station. When I wake up at 1000 hours and look around the garden plot that I've sneaked into, I see a neighbour standing by the fence. He is a man of about 70 years of age.

I try to explain to him how I've come to be there. He stops me with a wave of his hand and asks me what the situation is. I can't tell him anything that he doesn't already know. But he is able to tell me that the German troops in the Ruhr pocket have surrendered.

I say goodbye, and the old man picks up his watering can and waters the hotbeds. Life goes on!

I am able to travel further into Berlin by rail that evening.

After going through Grünau, Adlershof and Treptow, the train comes to a halt. No one can say if or when the train will get moving again. The transport links in the capital of the Reich have been interrupted in several locations.

20 April: Day has dawned. The train starts moving. My watch says 06.35. I notice that we aren't heading north. The city centre has probably been so heavily bombed that it'll be impossible to get through.

The train arrives in Spandau at 11.35. We are asked to get off. It seems that this will be the end of the journey. I can't just stick around where I am, so I decide to visit my Uncle Hermann. He lives right by the Have, opposite Siemensstadt. It takes me two hours to get to his home.

My aunt and uncle are surprised by my arrival. They are just as exhausted as I am. They have been sitting in the cellar night after night for weeks and have been hoping that they'll be spared the worst of the bombing. Their son Wolfgang is still missing.

We go upstairs from the cellar. My aunt places some bread and a piece of sausage on the table for me. I eat a slice of bread and leave the sausage. My aunt no doubt means well, but there is no way I can accept the last sausage from their limited rations.

I say goodbye that afternoon. We wish each other all the best. We all know that this farewell could well be the last. Soviet artillery are shelling the northern part of the city.

I stand on the road that leads from Spandau to the north, not quite knowing what I should do. The area seems to be deserted. The residents hardly emerge from the cellars any more. I hear a vehicle engine behind me. It is a truck! The driver gives me a lift, and I am in Velten-Hohenschöpping half an hour later.

I am given accommodation in the barracks there. The room in which I have my camp bed is occupied by 12 officers. All of them are more or less severely wounded. Most of them, like me, have experienced the catastrophe undergone by the 4. Armee in East Prussia and owe their survival to the fact that they were wounded in time.

Very little is said. It is clear to everyone that this war is lost. There is no doubt that it is only a matter of days or hours before Ivan is on our doorstep. Ivan will remember the trouble he's had with us. He will remember the enormous casualties he's suffered when he decided to take us on.

I lie on my bed and stared at the ceiling. It is nightmarish to have to lie there and do nothing apart from wait for imminent disaster.

A second lieutenant is summoned at 2100 hours. When he returns for his pistol, we learn from him that he will be accompanying a pioneer unit to blow up a canal bridge a few kilometres to the north-east. And then he is gone. The system of command and obedience is still being adhered to, even at this late stage. If I had received this order, I would have obeyed as well, and so too would every man in these barracks.

Another second lieutenant is summoned at 2300 hours. He too disappears into the night with a mission to carry out. We never see him again.

21 April: The hours go by slowly. According to the Führer's order, no soldier is allowed to leave the capital of the Reich, not even if he is wounded!

The explosions of artillery shells have got closer. The windowpanes are vibrating. I've been thinking the whole night long about what I'll do once the Reich enters its final hours and there are no longer any orders. I will try to escape to the west on my own! I won't wait until fate, in the form of a Russian, knocks on the door of these barracks!

I am summoned to the orderly room at 20.30. Now it is my turn, I think. Fate has caught up with me. I am informed that I will be leaving Berlin early the next day with a group of wounded soldiers and heading in the direction of Schleswig-Holstein. My destination will be Fredericia, in Denmark. I can't believe it at first.

22 April: It is a Sunday. I leave the barracks area of the Velten-Hohenschöpping camp shortly before 0500 hours with 20 wounded or disabled soldiers. We proceed along the road that leads to Veiten. We come to a stop at an anti-tank obstacle. I look back towards Henningsdorf. I can see movement in the terrain 300 metres to the south. It is Ivan! Soviet infantry has just crossed the Henningsdorf–Veiten railway line and is moving to the west.

Workers are cycling towards us from Veiten. I stop them. 'Where are you going?'

'We're on our way to the steelworks in Henningsdorf!'

I invite the workers to look through the opening in the anti-tank barrier to the south. They probably know what it is they are looking at, but one of them still asks: 'What's going on?'

'That's Ivan. No question.'

'So, what should we do now?'

'Go home. The war is over for you!'

Only hesitantly do the steelworkers get back on their bikes. I can tell from the expressions on their faces that they still can't quite believe what they've just seen with their own eyes.

I order my group of men to increase the speed of their march. We turn west as we go through Veiten, and, via Marwitz, we reach the village of Eichstädt. I get us to pause there for a moment. It is clear to me that we won't be able to elude the motorised Russian forces if we continue on foot. But luck is on our side. An open truck catches up with us beyond Eichstädt. I wave. The driver is happy to give us a lift.

We drive rapidly through Vehlefanz and Schwante to Kremmen. To my surprise, we are no longer heading west but rather north. I knock on the roof of the driver's cab. The truck comes to a halt.

'What is it?' asks the driver.

'What's your destination?' I ask.

'I have to get to Neustrelitz today.'

I'm not entirely sure about going in that direction, but for now it is more important to get away from Berlin. To our west lies the Rhinluch. Somewhere there in the mist is Fehrbellin, where the Great Elector defeated the Swedes to the south-west of Hakenberg in 1675 and thereby made the whole of Europe sit up and take notice. War was much more straightforward at that time. Now everything is out of proportion. It is no longer a case of defeating the enemy. Instead, it is about destroying him altogether, even if he has laid down his arms. This is a clear step backwards in the history of humanity.

We enter Neustrelitz at noon. We don't go any further today. I take my wounded men to the local Wehrmacht barracks instead.

23 April: I try to find transportation for my men early in the morning. Once again, we are in luck. There is a truck driver who is prepared to take us with him.

We drive west via Mirow, go around the southern side of Lake Müritz and reach Goldberg at 1100 hours. There is a lot of traffic on the roads, most of it heading west. The weather is good.

The countryside in Mecklenburg is beautiful. It would be a good place to visit in times of peace. How many spots have I had similar thoughts about during this war?

We've escaped the Russians. It is a satisfying feeling. But no sooner have I thought this than I hear fire from the onboard weaponry of low-flying aircraft in front of us. The truck driver hasn't yet noticed the approaching danger. I desperately knock on the roof of the driver's cab to try to bring the vehicle to a stop. We need to jump off as soon as possible.

But it is too late! The fighter-bombers have got closer. The tracer bullets lance towards us. I throw myself flat on the truck-bed.

The moment of horror is over as quickly as it began. Nothing happened to our truck, but many on the road in front of us have been killed.

We drive on. We keep gazing towards the sky and the horizon, and we arrive in Bad Kleinen, which lies by Lake Schwerin, in the early afternoon without incident. We are given a spot to sleep and some rations in the local Wehrmacht barracks, and in the evening we learn that Field Marshal Model shot himself a few days after the surrender of his troops in the Ruhr pocket. I admire the determination of this man. He was the master of his own fate right up until his death!

24 April: We are transported by truck to Schwerin, on the south-west shore of Lake Schwerin. The garrison is like a colony of bees that has been stirred up. Officers are issuing orders to all the men there regardless of whether they wear military or civilian clothing and regardless of whether they are young or old. Anyone whose papers aren't in order is put to work.

I am unable to find a means of transport for the continuation of our journey. We have to spend the night in Schwerin.

25 April: We leave Schwerin early in the morning in an open truck. After a few kilometres, I see a town sign by the side of the road: Gadebusch.

It was here that Theodor Körner fell in action in 1813 as a member of the Lützow Free Corps. He and his comrades sought to free Prussia – or whatever might have been understood to be Germany at that time – from Napoleon and the French. But times have changed. We simply want to survive!

We drive through the residential areas of Lübeck at noon. The city has been bombed to pieces.

We arrive in Eutin! Our truck has reached its destination. We get out. We won't be going any further today, so we make preparations to spend the night.

I go outside again after nightfall. I can hear anti-aircraft guns firing in the distance. The noise probably comes from the Bay of Kiel.

A first lieutenant from my march group approaches me. 'Do you really think we'll still make it to Fredericia?'

'I know as much as you do. Do you have any suggestions how to proceed in this rather unmanageable situation?'

He doesn't, so he changes the subject. 'Did you notice the grey figures in stripes who were shuffling along beside the road in a long line while we were driving from Schwerin to here? Did you notice their emaciated and expressionless faces?'

'I did,' I answer. 'I was horrified and still am!'

He continues: 'Were you aware that there were concentration camps? There are some people who claim that they didn't know about them!'

'I don't claim not to have known about them!' I reply. 'But what I didn't know was that the prisoners in those camps had been so maltreated that all that was left of them were human wrecks. Until now, I'd had a completely different, and obviously false, idea of what a concentration camp was for. I'd always thought that the people held, or concentrated, there were those who through agitation or deeds posed a threat to the existence of the state or, later, to the combat troops. Therefore I thought it right that such people be removed from the community. It would be unacceptable that we at the front should risk our lives while being sabotaged from behind. But I also think that prisoners should be treated humanely. What we've just seen is disgraceful!'

'Our enemies won't believe us if we say what you've just said. And you've only spoken of the political prisoners, not the Jews. Unbelievable things have apparently happened to them. We're in for a lot of trouble!'

Deep in thought, I return to my accommodation and lie down on my mattress on the floor. I try to put the faces of the prisoners out of my head, albeit in vain.

26 April: We drive through the scenic lake district around Plön in the early hours of the morning. From the loading platform of our truck, I look out at the wide grassy areas populated here and there by trees. It is a splendid sight. I try to take in the beauty of my surroundings and notice that I am unintentionally conducting an assessment of the terrain in accordance with the requirements of infantry combat. I am identifying concealed approaches, firing ranges and outflanking possibilities. This is a mode of thinking that I've slipped into several times while on leave. The war will come to an end at some point. But will we, who have been looking at our surroundings exclusively from a military perspective over the course of the last few years, ever be able to break free from this fixation?

The residential areas of Kiel are in ruins. The superstructures of sunken ships protrude from the water in the harbour area. The faces of the people in the city are etched with fear and hopelessness.

We leave Kiel and travel slowly to the west, arriving in Büdelsdorf, near Rendsburg, in the afternoon. This is where First Lieutenant Kruse, one of the officers in our march group, lives. He invites us to pause for a rest at his parents' house. We gratefully accept this offer.

27 April: The British have entered Bremen. We have no idea what will happen next. Our march orders state that we are to go to Fredericia. We don't know whether these orders are still valid under the changing circumstances, so we decide to wait in Büdelsdorf for the time being and see how the rapidly escalating situation develops.

28 April: Soldiers of all arms of the service move alone and in small groups along the roads to the north and south. It is clear that no form of organisation or leadership exists any longer.

29 April: The relief attack led by General Wenck in the western outskirts of Berlin has failed, and it is said that the Americans have entered Augsburg.

30 April: The German troops in Italy capitulated yesterday.

1 May: We decide to fall back to the north and are transported by truck to Flensburg via Schleswig.

We reach the German–Danish border at 1800 hours. I speak to the commander of the border guard unit, a first lieutenant. He advises me not to continue on into Denmark in the current situation. The sentiment of the Danes is not just unfriendly but actually hostile.

2 May: The High Command of the Wehrmacht announces: 'The Führer has fallen at the head of the heroic defenders of the capital of the Reich.' In fact, Hitler shot himself on 30 April 1945.

Grand Admiral Dönitz has taken over the leadership of the Reich!

The death of Hitler elicits no reaction from those around me. There is no applause. No one is impressed.

The German troops who are fighting against the Red Army continue to put up resistance. They enable as many people as possible to flee to the west. My comrades and I discus the situation and decide unanimously to head south again.

We leave Flensburg and proceed in the direction of Schleswig, arriving at the airbase in Jagel at noon. We've had enough of trying to escape our fate on the roads. The airbase commandant assigns us barracks accommodation. I am at the end of my tether and fall asleep before sunset.

3 May: Fighting is still taking place in Berlin. We know, reluctantly, that surrender is inevitable.

4 May: On the radio was the following announcement from the High Command of the Wehrmacht: 'The battle for the capital of the Reich has come to an end. In an unparalleled heroic struggle, troops from all branches of the Wehrmacht and from all units of the Volkssturm remained true to their oath of allegiance and fought hard until their final breath.'

5 May: A ceasefire is agreed with Montgomery's troops. The spearhead units of the British Army reach the main access road to the airbase in Jagel in the afternoon.

Some British armoured reconnaissance cars come to a stop in front of us. The crews huddled inside them don't quite know what to do. They are surrounded by us, and we are still fully armed. The boys from Great Britain attempt to defuse the strange atmosphere with wide smiles.

7 May: The Wehrmacht also concede victory to the Soviet Union. It is clear when I converse with my comrades that the surrender to the Russians gets under our skin much more than that to the Western powers.

Nevertheless, we regard the coordinated military effort of the Western Allies with the Soviets as a betrayal of Europe. It isn't possible to assess the full extent of what has happened. I can tell that even those among us who are usually powerfully eloquent are at a loss for words!

9 May: I've just come back from the commander's office and enter the accommodation barracks. Officers and men stand near the doorway. They wear grave expressions. I can hear the announcement on the radio in another room: 'Weapons on all fronts were laid down at midnight. On the order of the grand admiral, the Wehrmacht has ceased what has become a hopeless struggle. With that, almost six years of honourable fighting has come to an end. The Wehrmacht is at this final stage outgunned in the face of overwhelming superior forces. The unparalleled performance at the front and in the Fatherland will eventually be recognised in the judgement of history. The achievements and sacrifices of German combatants on land, at sea, and in the air cannot fail to be noticed even by our enemies. The Wehrmacht commemorates our comrades who have fallen in battle. The dead require of us that we demonstrate unconditional loyalty, obedience and discipline to a Fatherland that is bleeding from countless wounds!'

And that is the end of the final Wehrmacht communiqué. Oppressive silence reigns.

The second lieutenant next to me turns away. He has tears in his eyes. I also struggle to maintain my composure. The corporal opposite me gazes in my direction without a word. It seems that he is looking straight through me. His expression indicates utter disbelief.

The circle of listeners dissipates. A young captain pushes his way past me through the narrow corridor of the barracks and heads towards the exit. With his hand on the handle of the door, he glances back and says: 'Well, gentlemen, that's that, then!'

His words are full of despair, disappointment, bitterness and much more. His sarcasm doesn't go down well with me. I feel empty inside. I go outside. I want to be on my own.

How did things begin? Hitler had addressed the Reichstag on 1 September 1939: 'We have been returning fire since 05.45! From now on, bombs will be answered with bombs!'

And now, after almost six years of war of the kind that has never before been seen in the history of humanity, we get the words 'that's that, then'.

In between then and now, the fates of men and entire peoples have lain in the balance. Many of good faith have died: Jupp Reinardy, comrades from the fusilier battalion, and many others who cannot be named here but whose deaths nevertheless carry the same weight.

I find it difficult to organise my thoughts.

On my way back to the accommodation, I remember something from my adolescence. Surrounded by Brandenburgian Prussian standards, a blue flag cloth had attracted my attention. It was the company flag of the foot regiment of Colonel Hillebrand von Kracht from the year 1626. On it had been inscribed:

> Live steadily
> No misfortune
> For ever

My subconscious always internalised these words. The full brunt of everything that has happened brings them back to my conscious mind. I will live by them!

That was how they were, those who went before us ...

Question of the dead

I awoke, I sensed the door opening
Then my dead friend came in to me

The horror rose up in my throat
I spoke to him, he paid no attention

I asked: 'What disturbs your rest?
My dearest friend, what do you want me to do?'

He did not perceive my affection.
He looked right past me, strange and afar

And asked insistently yet soundlessly:
'Where is the front? Where is my battalion?'

(From Münchhausen's *Beeren-Auslese*)

While preserving elementary human and soldierly virtues, the generations that follow are duty-bound to ensure that soldiers never again finds themselves in the terrible situation of being crushed between the millstones of order and obedience!

Karl Knoblauch

Comrades

Arnold, Major – commander of Fallschirm-Panzerfüsilierbataillon 2 'Hermann Göring' (November 1944).

Bader, Master Sergeant – platoon leader in Fallschirm-Panzerfüsilierbataillon 2 'Hermann Göring' (November 1944).

Badorrek, Emil, Squadron Leader – German Cross in Gold, Knight's Cross of the Iron Cross with Oak Leaves. Commander of Fernaufklärergruppe 3, shot down and killed over Krakow 26.12.1944. Buried in the Krakow Military Cemetery.

Baer, Bern von, Lieutenant Colonel – Knight's Cross of the Iron Cross with Oak Leaves. Chief of staff of Fallschirm-Panzerkorps 'Hermann Göring'.

Bekemacker, Sergeant – leader of the flak platoon of Fallschirm-Panzerfüsilierbataillon 2 'Hermann Göring' (November 1944).

Bittrich, Wilhelm, SS-General – German Cross in Gold, Knight's Cross of the Iron Cross with Oak Leaves and Swords. Commander of II. SS-Panzerkorps.

Böttcher, Heinrich, Captain – commander of Fallschirm-Panzerpionierbataillon 'Hermann Göring'.

Ehlen, Master Sergeant – orderly officer of Fallschirm-Panzerfüsilierbataillon 2 'Hermann Göring' (November 1944).

Felician, Franz, Flight Sergeant – 4.(F)/14, later Aufklärungsgruppe 3, shot down and killed on 26.12.1944 above Krakow. Buried in the Krakow Military Cemetery.

Glück, Sergeant Major – leader of the mortar platoon of Fallschirm-Panzerfüsilierbataillon 2 'Hermann Göring' (November 1944).

Göring, Hermann, Reich Marshal – Commander-in-Chief of the Luftwaffe, suicide on 15.10.1946 while in American captivity in Nuremberg.

Gross, Second Lieutenant – signal officer of Fallschirm-Panzerfüsilierbataillon 2 'Hermann Göring' (November 1944).

Grün, Werner, Major – quartermaster of Fallschirm-Panzerkorps 'Hermann Göring'.

Heidenreich, Master Sergeant – platoon leader in Fallschirm-Panzerfüsilierbataillon 2 'Hermann Göring' (November 1944).

Kalff, First Lieutenant – leader of the 3rd Company of Fallschirm-Panzerfüsilierbataillon 2 'Hermann Göring'.

Kleine-Sextro, Franz-Josef, Second Lieutenant – orderly officer at the headquarters of Fallschirm-Panzerkorps 'Hermann Göring'.

Klingbeil, Werner, Captain – commander of the 5th Company of Fallschirm-Panzerfüsilierbataillon 2 'Hermann Göring', missing in action in Graudenz in February 1945.

Klodt, Second Lieutenant – platoon leader in Fallschirm-Panzerfüsilierbataillon 12 'Hermann Göring' (November 1944).

Kluge, Waldemar, Colonel – Knight's Cross of the Iron Cross. Commander of Fallschirm-Panzergrenadierregiment 4 'Hermann Göring'.

Knoblauch, Karl, First Lieutenant – German Cross in Gold. Radfahrschwadron 195 (95. Infanteriedivision), 4.(F)/14, I./Fallschirmjägerregiment 16(Ost), Fallschirm-Panzerfüsilierbataillon 2 'Hermann Göring'.

Kruse, Gerhard, First Lieutenant – Fallschirm-Panzeraufklärungsabteilung 'Hermann Göring'.

Küchel, Oskar, Second Lieutenant – orderly officer of Fallschirm-Panzerfüsilierbataillon 2 'Hermann Göring', missing in action in East Prussia in 1945.

Lehmann, Hans-Georg, First Lieutenant – German Cross in Gold, Knight's Cross of the Iron Cross, commander of Fallschirmkorpssturmbataillon 'Hermann Göring', missing in action in East Prussia in October 1944.

Lehmann, Wolfgang, Pilot Officer – 9. Luftwaffenfelddivision, Fliegerregiment 71.

Lingrön, Heinz, First Lieutenant – Fallschirm-Panzerfüsilierbataillon 2 'Hermann Göring', missing in action in East Prussia in December 1944.

Majer, Hans von, First Lieutenant, then Captain – Knight's Cross of the Iron Cross. Commander of the 2nd Company of Fallschirmjägerregiment 16, then commander of Fallschirmjägerregiment 27. Died 18.09.1983.

Meyer, Master Sergeant – platoon leader in Fallschirm-Panzerfüsilierbataillon 2 'Hermann Göring' (November 1944).

Model, Walter, Field Marshal – Knight's Cross of the Iron Cross with Oak Leaves, Swords, and Diamonds. Commander of 9. Armee, Commander-in-Chief West, commander of Heeresgruppe B, committed suicide in the Ruhr pocket on 21.04.1945.

Naumann, First Lieutenant – medical officer of Fallschirm-Panzerfüsilierbataillon 2 'Hermann Göring', whereabouts unknown.

Ortlieb, Sergeant – platoon leader in Fallschirm-Panzerfüsilierbataillon 2 'Hermann Göring' (November 1944).

Planert, Friedrich, First Lieutenant – 2nd Company of Fallschirm-Panzergrenadierregiment 3 'Hermann Göring', killed in action in East Prussia 17.01.1945.

Presber, Peter, Pilot Officer – 4.(F)/14, later Jagdegeschwader 3, shot down and killed on 22.04.1944 over the Reich. Grave in Schlotheim/Thüringen, Communal Cemetery.

Preuss, Captain – commander of the 1st Company of Fallschirm-Panzerfüsilierbataillon 2 'Hermann Göring', killed in action in Girnen, East Prussia, on 19.01.1945.

Prikowitsch, Sergeant – platoon leader in Fallschirm-Panzerfüsilierbataillon 2 'Hermann Göring' (November 1944).

Quentin, Sergeant – platoon leader in Fallschirm-Panzerfüsilierbataillon 2 'Hermann Göring' (November 1944).

Rapp, Second Lieutenant – commander of the 2nd Company of Fallschirm-Panzerfüsilierbataillon 2 'Hermann Göring', missing in action in East Prussia in 1945.

Reinardy, Josef (Jupp), Pilot Officer – German Cross in Gold. 4.(F)/14; later Aufklärungsgruppe 3, shot down and killed on 26.12.1944 over Krakow. Grave in Krakow Military Cemetery.

Reitz, Karl, Corporal – 2nd Company of Fallschirmjägerregiment 16, killed in action at Annahof, south-west of Gumbinnen, on 22.10.1944. Burial place to the north-west of the rail and road crossing west of Annahof (3 kilometres to the south-west of Gumbinnen).

Sandrock, Hans, Major – Knight's Cross of the Iron Cross. Commander of Fallschirm-Sturmgeschützabteilung 2 'Hermann Göring'.

Scheler, Sergeant – platoon leader in Fallschirm-Panzerfüsilierbataillon 2 'Hermann Göring' (November 1944).

Schirmer, Gerhard, Lieutenant Colonel – Knight's Cross of the Iron Cross with Oak Leaves. Commander of Fallschirmjägerregiment 16.

Schmalz, Wilhelm, Major General – German Cross in Gold, Knight's Cross of the Iron Cross with Oak Leaves. Commander of Fallschirm-Panzerkorps 'Hermann Göring'. Died 14.03.1983.

Schneider, Gert, Second Lieutenant – signal officer of Fallschirm-Panzerfüsilierbataillon 2 'Hermann Göring', missing in action in East Prussia in 1945.

Schröder, Sergeant – platoon leader in Fallschirm-Panzerfüsilierbataillon 2 'Hermann Göring' (November 1944).

Schweim, Heinz-Herbert, Major – Knight's Cross of the Iron Cross. First general staff officer of Fallschirm-Panzerfüsilierbataillon 2 'Hermann Göring'.

Siller, Gerhard (Gert), Flight Sergeant – German Cross in Gold. 4.(F)/14, later reconnaissance observer in Aufklärungsgruppe. 3, shot down and killed on 26.12.1944 over Krakow. Grave in Krakow Military Cemetery.

Söth, Wilhelm, Colonel – German Cross in Gold. Temporary commander of Fallschirm-Panzergrenadierdivision 2 'Hermann Göring' (autumn 1944).

Staguhn, Master Sergeant – commander of the 4th Company of Fallschirm-Panzerfüsilierbataillon 2 'Hermann Göring'.

Staufenberg, Claus Graf Schenk von, Colonel – first general staff officer of 10. Panzerdivision (Africa); later staff officer to the headquarters of the Ersatzheer (Replacement Army). Court-martialled and shot on 20.07.1944.

Stein, Gerd, Second Lieutenant – I Battalion of Fallschirmjägerregiment 16, killed in action in East Prussia on 21.10.1944.

Tatenhorst, Master Sergeant – platoon leader in Fallschirm-Panzerfüsilierbataillon 2 'Hermann Göring'.

Teusen, Hans, Captain (1944) – Knight's Cross of the Iron Cross. Commander of I. Battalion of Fallschirmjägerregiment 16.

Tischler, Sergeant – company commander in Fallschirm-Panzerfüsilierbataillon 2 'Hermann Göring' (November 1944).

Trippens, Erich, Sergeant – platoon leader in the 2nd Company of Fallschirm-Panzerfüsilierbataillon 2 'Hermann Göring'.

Truckenmüller, Fritz, Captain – headquarters of the Fallschirm-Panzergrenadierdivision 2 'Hermann Göring', missing in action in East Prussia in January 1945.

Walther, Erich, Colonel (Major General) – German Cross in Gold, Knight's Cross of the Iron Cross with Oak Leaves and Swords. Commander of Fallschirm-Panzergrenadierdivision 2 'Hermann Göring'. Starved to death in the Soviet Buchenwald concentration camp on 26.12.1947.

Wenck, Walther, General of Panzer Troops – Knight's Cross of the Iron Cross. Chief of staff of I. Panzerarmee (1943), chief of staff of Heeresgruppe Südukraine (1944), chief of operations at the High Command of the German Army (1944), commander of 12. Armee (1945).

Wilshues, Sergeant – platoon leader in the 4th Company of Fallschirm-Panzerfüsilierbataillon 2 'Hermann Göring'.

Wolf, August, Captain – commander of Fallschirm-Panzerfüsilierbataillon 2 'Hermann Göring'.

Acknowledgements

My thanks go to those who have helped me to check dates, locations and details on personnel, and those who have lent me photos and maps, or who have offered me good advice:

Erich Busch, Friedrich Hucke, Burkhard Mahler, Rudolf Marwan-Schlosser, Otto Merk, Helmut Michel, Alfred Otte, Joachim Paul, Arnold von Roon, Gerhard Schirmer, Karl-Heinz Schmeelke, Heinz-Herbert Schweim, Helma Wolf.

THROUGH FIRE & SKY